WITHDRAWN

THE BIBLE
ON BROADWAY

THE BIBLE ON BROADWAY

A SOURCE BOOK FOR MINISTERS,
EDUCATORS, LIBRARIANS, AND
GENERAL READERS

By Arthur T. Buch

Archon Books
1968

SBN: 208 00271 5
Library of Congress Catalog Card Number: 68-9809
Printed in the United States of America

TO THE MEMORY OF
MY MOTHER

Contents

Foreword

Scholars have had an on-going interest in identifying relationships and in classifying knowledge. In this volume, Dr. Buch has systematically brought together, even though he has not intended it to be a completely exhaustive review of all plays and motion pictures, the specific relationships of Biblical concepts to the basic ideas and values contained in many of to-day's theatrical productions. This is a novel approach, and the fact that it has continued effectively as a theme for group meetings and for a newspaper feature for several years gives tangible support to the fundamental urge of people to link man's thoughts to modern drama.

The book is divided conveniently into various aspects of life —the home and the family, work and the search for money, education and its many facets, man as a social animal, and man and his recreation and religion. In a free and popular but controlled style, the author has completed a most useful task in showing how Biblical values are closely interwoven in our way of living, in simplifying academic research of the theatre and religion, and in projecting some aspects of the philosophy and mystery of life.

The volume should have great usefulness not only to students and others concerned with the field of the drama, but also to general laymen, who spend considerable time in the theatre. The ministerial profession, as well as educators generally, should find an endless number of nuggets in this volume directly related to their daily activities. Librarians particularly should find this collection of comments about plays and motion pictures, in the light of the Bible, a source book for themselves and for their readers. Dr. Buch has contributed a work that should be, especially in these days of difficulty and strife, most timely, since the wisdom of the Bible is so needed.

Maurice F. Tauber

Preface

This book is an outcome of a number of years' experience on the part of the author as lecturer, college instructor, and newspaper feature writer on the subject of the Bible and the contemporary theatre. Its purpose is to make available a certain amount of basic material (one hundred and thirty articles of approximately three hundred words each, written on today's plays and movies in the light of the Bible), in connection with topics listed in the table of contents, which are necessarily a part of a philosophy of life. The material thus organized represents the Biblical point of view held by the author and presented to his classes, audiences, and reading public. The selection of the pieces on the theatre has not been confined to those plays and movies which agree with this point of view, nor to those which are opposed. Rather, the selection was made practically at random with no consideration given to what must and must not be included. Some plays or movies, therefore, are omitted, which might well have been included, and some are included which, by comparison with others, do not appear to be that significant.

Furthermore, it was not intended that this book include a reference to all theatrical material of the last few years. Rather, the overriding purpose was to present a philosophy of life which can be identified in theatrical productions, as in everyday life, but which may not be observed, except as specific instances of occurrence in a number of modern plays and motion pictures which are cited, analyzed and discussed. With insight into the extent to which Biblical philosophy is demonstrated in the drama of life, as portrayed in the theatre, the reader may enjoy new plays and films, and proceed, with renewed vigor, to greater fulfillment in life.

It is in place here to point out that when I mention books of the Bible, I am referring to those commonly called the Old

Testament. To be sure, other students of the Drama and Religion—especially Christian theologians—have produced fine insights in this area by referring to the New Testament.

The following chapters, it should be noted, are arranged logically and topically, not necessarily in an order of strict sequence. After Introduction A explaining the origin and meaning of the title and subject, "The Bible on Broadway" and Introduction B, listing a set of principles on the nature and relationship of the Bible and the Theatre to serve as background for the whole work, Chapter I deals with home life and the need for love; Chapter II concerns itself with the economic interests of man and their encounters with his morality; Chapter III raises the issue of education for a better world; Chapter IV calls attention to man's ethical goals and his dual nature; Chapter V relates itself to the matter of man's recreation, and the Drama as a special part of this interest; Chapter VI is concerned with the matter of life, its purpose and God; an Epilogue; and Appendix A contains a list of the plays and movies discussed and Appendix B, a list of Books of the Bible with the verses cited in this book.

At the beginning of each chapter is a brief introductory statement. These statements are intended to orient the reader to the areas covered by the material presented. Also, before each article dealing with a specific Biblical text and modern play or movie, there is a statement which serves as a continuity linking the articles together in a more or less integrated fashion, for the purpose of indicating the overall philosophy for modern living which is suggested by "The Bible on Broadway".

For permission to reprint material which had previously appeared in their respective newspapers, the writer hereby expresses his appreciation to the publishers of the *Passaic Herald News*, and the *Newark Star-Ledger*.

My thanks are expressed also to the New York Newspaper Reporters Association for the right to reprint an article which appeared in "Byline".

I am most grateful to Congregation Shaare Zedek and to its Sisterhood for affording me the opportunity to develop my project, "The Bible on Broadway".

My thanks to Professor Irlene Roemer Stephens, Professor and

Chief Librarian, Richmond College of the City of New York, stem from my recognition of her valuable suggestions and her invaluable encouragement.

I thank my loyal friend, Dr. Maurice F. Tauber, Melvil Dewey Professor of Library Service at Columbia University, without whom this book would not have seen the light of day. A constant source of encouragement, enlightenment and practical help, Dr. Tauber has proven himself to be the true librarian who loves books and the making of them.

In thanking Dr. Tauber, I am thinking also of his late, sainted wife, Rose, who expressed a keen and friendly interest in my efforts.

Introduction

A

This book is replete with introductions. Each chapter begins with a clearly marked introduction. Every one of the articles dealing with a particular play or movie has some introductory remarks of its own. There is need for this opening, general Introduction A, nevertheless. Here the questions, What is the meaning of the phrase, "The Bible on Broadway"? and What are its origin and history? should be answered.

An article which was written for "Byline" (vol. 15 no. 1), the annual magazine published by the New York Newspaper Reporters Association had this precise purpose, namely to answer the questions of the meaning and origin of our title, and it is accordingly repeated here.

"The Bible on Broadway"

So now I, too, am a member of what may very well be the most aging profession in the world—that of writing for newspapers.

This membership has come to me not so much because of my recent appointment as one of the chaplains for the NRA. No, the keys to the Duchy of Newspaperdom have been handed to me not through my "heavenly" qualifications, but by reason of my own blood, sweat and tears as a working writer. You see, I am now writing for newspapers a weekly series of articles, entitled "The Bible on Broadway".

At this point you might very well be confused. How, first of all, could I transfer from the First to the Fourth Estate, without leaving the Clergy? In the second place, what has the Bible to do with Broadway in the first place?

Answers to both these questions have their origin several years ago when the television quiz programs were under investigation. I was deeply troubled—as I am sure you were—by the impression that was being left in the minds and hearts of people everywhere of America's degradation.

Morally and culturally, American society as reflected in our TV programs, our theatrical fare, our literature and art appeared to have hit bottom.

Gen. David Sarnoff felt prompted to issue a statement in defense of the TV industry. He pointed out that there was much good in its programs that was being overlooked while its occasional derelictions were being overly stressed. It struck me that what he was saying about TV applied to other aspects of American culture as well, particularly to theatrical productions.

Without necessarily resting on his conviction that the good outweighed the bad in American cultural activity, I saw further implications in General Sarnoff's declaration. Audiences needed to be sensitized more and more to the positive qualities of the entertainment and cultural media. In addition, through such increased public sensitivity producers would be encouraged to provide ever more of the fine, and less of the sordid.

Here is where questions arise. If the exemplary aspects of TV are not being recognized, what is the reason for such a lack of appreciation? Similarly, and further, if the theatre, including in this term the legitimate stage, on and off Broadway as well as the moving pictures, has large measures of goodness, truth and beauty which are unappreciated, how are we to change this situation?

All in all, what should be done to encourage and condone the good, and to discourage and condemn the unsavory in the American cultural pattern?

These are serious and pressing questions—serious for the survival of the American Way of Life, and pressing for immediate and adequate answers. Indeed the simple truth is that the face that America shows the world affects seriously the future of democracy all over the globe.

Each American mature enough to ask "What can I do for my country?" ought to concern himself with answers to the above questions. Accordingly, I set myself to thinking about the matter.

Since the theatre in its broadest sense is a large aspect of

American culture—its expression as well as its creation—I saw the urgent importance of bringing the worthwhile elements in the American Theatre to the fore. Especially was this importance impressed on me when I realized how much Hollywood was involved in exporting American Life to the world, and how much Broadway with all its theatres meant to the modern drama.

Then the thought of the Bible came to me in this connection. Was not the Bible the basis of western civilization as far as morals are concerned? Why not use the Bible as guide and touchstone, as direction and goal in the matter of the cultural achievements of western society? Thus was born "The Bible on Broadway".

The birth of the idea accomplished, rearing it brought the usual difficulties of raising a child—albeit in this case a "brain" one. There was first the fact that the Bible, although the world's best seller, is not the world's best read book. Second was the current impression that "message-plays" must necessarily be dull and unpopular. What a combination! The Bible unknown, and Broadway (in the sense of theatre with an idea) unpopular!

Still, I was drawn to the project of a series of lectures on the Bible and the contemporary theatre. What if the Bible is not well known? Teach it! Plays with a message dull? All plays by reason of their being works of art have been created by their authors' selection and ordering of experience. As such, plays are proponents of ideas—and certainly they are not meant to be uninteresting.

Thus fortified, I turned to the subject of the Bible and the contemporary theatre and found it indeed appealing and full of interesting nuances.

That there are spiritual, even religious ideas, in the contemporary theatre should be no cause for wonderment. It is well known that the drama had its origin in religion. The Greeks, the Romans, as well as the early Hebrews, all had forms of the drama which among the first two developed into our classical plays.

In the Middle Ages, it was the Church in the Western World that produced the morality and mystery plays. With such a long history it is not surprising to find an affinity between the Bible and the Theatre.

Moreover, in our own day, the Bible has been recognized as furnishing many good scripts. Bosley Crowther, film critic of The New York Times, has written interestingly about this phenomenon. Unfortunately, the Biblical narrative has been commercialized so garishly and grievously in most instances that both the Bible and the drama have suffered. Suspect as these efforts may be, the fact remains that the association of Scriptures with scripts is not at all strange.

Based on the natural—although frequently unrecognized—relationship between the Bible and the drama, the Sisterhood of my Congregation Shaare Zedek sponsored (and still does) an annual series of monthly lecture sessions, entitled "The Bible on Broadway". At these gatherings, I lecture on an appropriate section of the Scriptures as it applies to some current play which is under consideration. Outstanding theatre personalities are our guests at these affairs.

Additionally, I taught a course which had the name "The Bible and the Contemporary Theatre" at the New School for Social Research.

Most recently I began to write a series of weekly articles of 300 words each under the general heading of "The Bible on Broadway". These articles are now being published in *The Passaic Herald News*, and *The Newark Star-Ledger*.

Here is an example of one of these articles:

To know how to read and write is basic for civilized living. Every one knows that reading, like writing and arithmetic, has to be acquired through learning. To read a book, for example, requires much training in the particular faculty known as "reading ability".

More and more is being studied and done about this ability in so-called reading clinics.

An ancient truth probably comes to the fore often even in the most modern psychologist's research in the field. It is that a knowledge of the mechanics of reading is not sufficient to understand what has been written. One needs an apperceptive mass with which to grasp the meaning of an author's words.

This mass of knowledge must include necessarily an emotional sensitivity. In other words, one must be spiritually literate if one is to appreciate literature with spiritual overtones.

The Bible certainly demands spiritual sensitivity on the part of its readers, if they would understand it well. This point is made beautifully in the play "Brigadoon" which justifiably enjoys many revivals, especially in our summer theatres.

The story tells of a purported miracle of the Scottish village, Brigadoon, which had disappeared mysteriously, but returns to this world for one day every hundred years.

Two American tourists happen upon Brigadoon on one of those days of its reappearance. Its villagers are about to celebrate a wedding.

Noting the strange dates recorded in the family Bible of those being married, the two Americans are introduced to an old teacher who seeks to explain the miracle suggested by the datings.

Of course, there are no full explanations to miracles. The most Brigadoon's teacher can do is reimpress all with the truth that to know how to read and understand is not a mechanical thing. How true! One must be spiritually literate to read the Book of Books and certainly the Book of Life.

B

The Final Report (February, 1966) of a "Conference on the Use of Printed and Audio-Visual Materials for Instructional Purposes" prepared by Maurice F. Tauber and Irlene Roemer Stephens, contains papers delivered at a two-day meeting at the School of Library Service, Columbia University, November 22–23, 1965. Distinguished leaders of educational thought and research had dealt with the matter of the use of other than "conventional" material—such as books—for the development of the art of teaching and the concomittant process of learning. Among these new "non-conventional" materials were mentioned such things as the media of television and moving pictures.

Recognizing the need for greater research in the use of these, one of the participating lecturers, Dr. Dwayne E. Huebner, suggested that there are aesthetic and moral values inherent in them which should be communicated to students. Not only teachers of elementary and adult students, but librarians must become aware of the principles by which these values can be transmitted.

What, however, is the situation with the ordinary instructor? "The teacher, too busy with his teaching to keep abreast of all new developments, needs someone nearby to scan these developments and to bring them to his attention. Likewise, he needs someone to help him develop the skills or to use the media and messages for him until he can develop the skills. The values to be realized in the classroom depend very heavily upon the materials and media which come into the teachers' field of attention." (p. 19)

Not only the teacher in the secular—and certainly in the religious—school, as well as the librarian, but ordinary laymen could profit by being provided with some general principles by which the moral and spiritual values of such media as the legitimate drama, television, radio and moving pictures could be better appreciated, and be neither misunderstood nor overlooked.

Since our book which deals with the relationship between the Bible and plays and movies mostly presented in the years 1963 and 1964 presents such spiritual values, the reader, be he educator or student or layman, is presented with the following set of principles to serve as a background for them.

I

1. The Bible is more than a theological treatise. It is a guide for the conduct of man's life.

2. Challenges to the Bible have not been ignored by it in the past. In some cases they were met head on; in some instances these challenges were anticipated and incorporated into the Biblical tradition.

3. The Bible is not just a library of books. It is also an interpretation, a view-point, a spirit, a tradition about life and its meaning.

4. The Bible is a development over centuries. That development as a "Biblical tradition" continues even in our day.

II

5. The Drama, aptly called "The Naked Image" by Clurman, is the liveliest, most life-like of the Arts.

6. In the Drama, not only the content of a theatrical produc-

tion, but its form has a spiritual message. Writing in another connection, Stanley Edgar Hyman in his "Standards: A Chronicle of Books for our Time," states it well: ". . . form as the ordering of disorder is a moral act".

III

7. In our day guidance and philosophy can be provided for mature, integrated living on the part of individuals as well as groups, as there is a revival of communication between religious and secular evaluations of the human condition.

8. The conceptions of the Bible as these have to do with ethics, culture, esthetics and religion can serve to put in proper perspective the problems and aspirations of modern man as reflected in the contemporary theatre.

9. A number of our leading thinkers maintain that the tone of our civilization is "existential with its emphasis on alienation or estrangement and even the death of God". It is this quality which they find conveyed in the plays of those whom they regard as characteristic of our generation, e.g. Pirandello, Brecht, Sartre.

Whether or not this condition is as universal as maintained, the fact is that the Bible has the power to assimilate this view of the world into its vision of the universe.

10. The purported, and in some cases, evident disregard of the Bible's values and insights does not mean that they are not valid.

A recapture of these can develop for the individual an integrated sense of values and purpose which would help him live through difficulties, and afford him a positive, spiritual focus for living.

*   *   *   *   *   *   *

The invention and use of the electric light had a great influence in heightening the effect of the theatre and its productions. A rediscovery and redirection of the values and truths of the Bible in keeping with the foregoing principles can help place in the proper light and afford direction for that most dramatic of all the creatures in the universe—Man himself.

THE BIBLE
ON BROADWAY

I

Love and Family Life

When A Home Is A Home—
It's A Blessing

For this first chapter we have selected the material which deals with aspects of the theatre and the Bible touching upon what may be considered a human being's primary interests. These are a person's concern for survival and happiness. This dual goal involves a process of developments which has been variously analyzed and evaluated. Freud, for example, has maintained that sex is the prime factor—frequently unconscious—in explaining human behavior. Religionists and a number of psychologists, such as Eric Fromm, have stressed this fundamental urge as a manifestation of love. Not a few sociologists advance the argument that family and home are the determining influences in human experience. No one would deny that "man born of woman" must necessarily be deeply concerned with parent-child relationships, with proper mating, with sex morals, with all those things that spell love, family, and honor.

A. FAMILY SPELLS FUTURE

A human being normally begins his or her life in a family situation. The parents most often are filled with joy at the birth of an offspring. Societies of nations—at least until the advent of the population explosion—were also pleased by the birth of the young. These represented the hope for the future. In a well-known play by Edward Albee there is expressed grave concern that Americans may be destroying this hope.

"Who's Afraid of Virginia Woolf?"
Text: They shall not labour in vain
Nor bring forth for terror;

> For they are the seed blessed of the Lord,
> And their offspring with them.
>
> —Isaiah 65:23

Edward Albee's play, "Who's Afraid of Virginia Woolf?" carries with it some challenging "ifs".

If the title of the drama sung occasionally as a ditty through the play means that Virginia Woolf is the symbol of an American intellectualism and cultural leadership that have failed, then we have reason to be concerned.

If the names of the two married couples of the cast have significance, then we Americans should be alert to their message. The names of one couple are George and Martha, and the names of the other two are Nick and Honey. George and Martha may remind us of the Washingtons, the Father of this country and his spouse. Nick and Honey are typical names of America's young people of the masses.

If the goings-on of the two couples visiting with each other are supposed to represent more than just an evening's experience of a history professor and his wife, who is the daughter of the President of the University, and a biology professor and his wife, then we have to take serious note of what transpired.

If the point of the story is that America's social and cultural life—even at its highest academic level—is beset with immorality and a loss of dignity and high purpose, then we have to face seriously the consequences of such continued debauchery of values.

The result must be, as Edward Albee puts its symbolically and dramatically, that the "kids", the future generations, are doomed, America itself must forfeit its future, and indeed, "the West . . . must eventually fall."

So does Edward Albee indirectly point up the blessing that is in store for the nation that does not forsake its highest moral goals. It is the blessing foreseen by the Prophet Isaiah:

> They shall not labour in vain
> Nor bring forth in terror.

If America will be shocked by and out of the prospects suggested by the adherance to the cult of Virginia Woolf, then it shall be "a seed blessed by the Lord". This is, indeed, the most challenging and crucial "if".

B. MORALS—AND THE LACK OF THEM

Whether dealt with seriously or in a lighter vein, the theme of marital infidelity is frequently handled in the contemporary theatre, as in one of Edward Chodorov's plays.

"Oh Men, Oh Women"

Text: Woe unto them that call evil good,
        and good evil . . .

—Isaiah 5:20

No civilized living is possible without standards and values of conduct. The mess in which people find themselves from time to time is the result of a failure to live by proper standards, or to judge on the basis of correct values.

The Prophet Isaiah succinctly stated the situation when he decried the confusion that must result from those whose way of life is based on wrong standards. "These", said the prophet, "change darkness into light and light into darkness". (Ch. 5, V. 10). When unsocial acts become the goal, while ethical conduct is degraded, then indeed has "bitter been changed into sweet, and sweet into bitter".

It is not only the wicked who so pervert values. The innocent frequently err in mistaking the good for evil, and the evil for good. This can come about in various ways. Sometimes it happens by forgetting the simple essentials of proper conduct and becoming so involved with sophistications, that there is a "muddying of the waters".

In Chodorov's play, "Oh Men, Oh Women", one sees a farcical situation that is reflected in a certain psychiatrist's office and private life when the hero, the psychiatrist, discovers to his surprise that one of his patients has been well acquainted with the young lady he is about to marry.

This farce has a message, along with funny moments. The mix-up first leads one of the characters in the play to exclaim: "Oh men, oh women! Is there any hope for you?"

The answer seems to be in the negative as long as there is a forgetting of the fundamental rules of proper conduct applying to men and women.

Let there be, however, a simple return to what is right and expected of men and women. Then the farce so often made of their relationships will be over.

C. CHURCHMEN—AND ENGLISHMEN

It is not only in the contemporary society that this phenomenon of marital infidelity has made its appearance. England in Henry Fielding's days, according to this author whose famous novel became a popular movie, was only too well familiar with it.

"Tom Jones"

Text: Ye shall therefore keep My Statutes, and
        Mine Ordinances, which if a man do,
        he shall live by them; I am the Lord.

—Leviticus 18:5

Near the middle of the eighteenth century Henry Fielding's classic novel, "Tom Jones", was published. Since it describes the life of Merrie England in the early part of that century, we may assume that Fielding knew of what he was writing.

What he wrote reveals an England whose way of life from the highest to the lowest in its society was not unmarred by immorality. Recently, this subject matter was transferred to the screen in a moving picture which won acclaim as the best film of the year.

What may impress the viewer of the movie as well as the reader of the novel, is that in the midst of all the ribaldry and lustiness which produce many a funny situation, there is the question of where was the Church of England through all .of this. Apparently, in spite of the many trappings of religion— churches, vestments, preachers, ministers, etc.—these had little effect on the lives of the people of that time.

In this regard, one of the most interesting scenes of the film takes place in a church where as a service is in progress there is an obvious lack of sincerity on the part of the congregation. Thus it is made clear that the fundamental principle of true religion calling for sincere application of its tenets to all aspects of living was frequently honored in the breach in those days of English history.

In sum, it is in a sense funny to find so much Bible in England with so little Bible in Englishmen. In a deeper sense from such a humorous disparity, a nation may laugh and laugh until tears come to the eyes.

D. NO HOME IS COMPLETE WITHOUT A BIBLE

Although it is possible to have the "Bible in England, and have so little of it in Englishmen", the Bible still must be accepted as the standard of morality for the Western World. What is needed is more devotion to it to have it function better. Certainly, no one will deny the needs for more adequate spiritual preparation for marriage. By indirection, Jean Kerr makes this point in her most delightful play.

"Mary, Mary"

Text: A woman of valour who can find?
        For her price is far above rubies.
        The heart of her husband doth trust in her . . .
        But a woman that feareth the Lord, she shall be
        praised.
                                        —Proverbs 31:10, 12, 30

"Mary, Mary, quite contrary." This phrase might very well have been in gifted playwright Jean Kerr's mind when she wrote her play which is presently a success on Broadway and also has been fashioned into a current movie. Naming her heroine Mary, the authoress titled her play, "Mary, Mary".

This stage "Mary" is also naturally referred to by doubling her name, as is done with her famous namesake, because she, like the girl of the rhyme, is so rambunctious and confounding. Particularly is she such to her husband. Matters reach such a state that the couple are in the process of being divorced when the play opens.

The events leading up to this point and what happens there-
after make "Mary, Mary" a comedy of errors. In the confusion described, it is not only the wife who appears
contrary, but the husband as well. An insight into the state of
affairs is furnished by the admission of the husband that he
married Mary because "she was so direct and straightforward
and said exactly what she meant". Now he argues that he wants
to divorce her because "she is so direct and straightforward and
said exactly what she meant". For her part, Mary explains: "He
was in love with me. Else why would I marry him?"
It is such kind of reactions that reveal why the marriage was
foundering. What was needed was far more thoughtfulness
about the meaning of marriage as a sacred, responsible institution in which a husband and wife live together.
In the play the husband is presented as a book publisher with
a large library at home. One wonders whether he had a Bible
in it. He and Mary would have been well advised to follow its
guide-lines, especially those of Proverbs, Chapter 31, verses 10
through 31.

E. IT'S THE SAME EVERYWHERE

Of course, the Bible as a spiritual guide means most to those
who follow the Judeo-Christian tradition of the West. For the
people who live in the East, their own sacred tradition can be
expected to substitute for the Bible. Actually, the teachings of
morality and ethics are fundamentally the same the world over,
even as the everyday experiences of married life are alike. Take,
for example, the "mother-in-law image" as theme in an Indian
picture.

"The Householder"

Text: From lack of spirit and hard work.
                                              —Exodus 6:9
        And they shall do the service of the Lord.
                                              —Numbers 8:11

In Biblical Hebrew, the word for "labor" is the same word
that means "religious services". The origin for this lies in the
root of the word which signifies to work for, hence to serve, then

particularly, the Lord. Thus, the ancient temple ritual dedicated to the Service of God is called "Avodah", while the same term is used for plain, common work.

In the light of this, an axiom of the Geeta, India's collection of spiritual principles, takes on added interest. It is the maxim that teaches, "Work is Worship". Nowhere in the Bible is there to be found a formulation precisely like the Indian motto, although in Hebrew, the word for "work" and "worship" is the same.

The similarity of the thought of associating work and worship, along with the different aspect of the idea in the Hebrew and Indian tradition is brought to mind by the motion picture, "The Householder". Indeed, the whole subject of similarities and differences among human societies is raised by this deceptively simple movie.

The film, based on the novel by R. Prauer Thabvala, tells of the life of a newly-wedded Indian householder. It arouses pathos and humour in an American audience which identifies easily with the hero.

In the question of the wife who asks, "What will I wear?", as in the husband's complaint, "My mother cooked differently", there is universal recognition. Let there be no doubt about it— a mother-in-law is a mother-in-law in all cultures.

Still it would be wrong to claim that all societies are the same, for there are obvious differences. What is not so obvious is how to appreciate these diverse yet similar human situations. This is something for householders and non-householders everywhere to ponder more and more in our rapidly shrinking world.

F. DOMINANCE OF MODERN WOMAN
1. As Wife

It is generally recognized that women in the Western World have achieved a higher status in society than previously. Indeed, many think that contemporary society finds women in control as wives and mothers, even in the general community. Two plays that deal with this theme stress in one case the dominance of woman as wife, and in the other instance the dominance of woman as mother.

"Oh Dad, Poor Dad, Mamma's Hung You in the Closet,
and I'm Feeling So Sad"

Text: The Lord God said: It is not good for man to be
        alone;
        I will make a fitting helper for him.

—Genesis 2:18

The origin of woman is explained by the Bible as related to
her purpose for being, namely to be a "fitting helper" for man.
A literal translation of the Hebrew phrase "fitting helper"
would be "a help against him". On this basis, a meaningful interpretation has developed to the effect that if a man is considered worthy, his wife is a "helper". If, however, he is not deemed
meritorious, then she is "against" him.

This interpretation applies not only to woman as man's wife
but also as the mother of his children. It refers also to her role
in society in general. A whole society may find its women are
influences either for good or for evil.

Furthermore, women, as sociologists informed us long ago,
may be the dominating factor as in a matriarchy, or they may
be subservient as in some patriarchal societies.

Now there has come along a brilliant young playwright,
Arthur Kopit, who tells us that in our modern age regardless
of whether our society be considered matriarchal or patriarchal,
woman controls man completely. She has him in her power and
will not let him go. Between his mother and his wife, man has
lost his independence.

This loss of freedom is always tragic but especially so for the
young adult. In fact, the situation is so trying that it appears
absurd and therefore funny. This explains the nature of Kopit's
play with the long title: "Oh Dad, poor Dad, Mamma's hung
you in the closet, and I'm feeling so sad".

If there be grounds to Mr. Kopit's thesis, then the question
is: What can our society do to be deemed meritorious enough
for its women not to be "against" but to be the "helpmates" of
their men?

This is a really good question.

Indeed, even if Mr. Kopit is not altogether right, it still is a
fundamental question.

2. As Mother

"Dear Me, the Sky is Falling"

Text: If any soul shall sin through error.

—Leviticus 4:8

A large question for theologians is: How can we speak of a "soul sinning"? By definition, a soul is the divine spark in man. It is part of the breath of God. How come, then, that this spiritual emanation from the Creator should fall into such grievous error as to sin?

To this question have come various answers from theologians. What may interest us now, however, is the approach of psychoanalysis to this problem. It has substituted the concept of "psyche" or "personality" for the idea of the "soul". Additionally, instead of "sin", psychoanalysts have advanced a scientific terminology for the illness of the psyche or the personality. This includes such terms as disoriented, insecure, over-possessive, dependent, etc., etc.

It is such words which the audience at a showing of the laugh and thought provoking play, "Dear me, the sky is falling," hears frequently. Gertrude Berg—nay, Molly Goldberg—plays the role of Mrs. Libby Hirsch, a suburban wife and mother whose conduct causes her daughter, husband, sister, intended son-in-law, and finally herself, a good deal of aggravation and concern.

Her daughter, Debbie, turns to Dr. Evans, a psychiatrist, for help. At first spoofing his efforts, Mrs. Hirsch is forced finally to "take from him", too!

The analysis? An over-possessive and commanding personality. Mrs. Hirsch is forced to accept this diagnosis and the prescription for cure. This is difficult for her to do and understand, for she knows that she only meant well.

Using its own phrases, psychoanalysis explains that a "good soul"—such as Mrs. Hirsch—"sins" precisely when she tries to be too good a "soul".

Does this mean that psychiatrists have all the answers? No. When Dr. Evans needs some plain warm-hearted friendliness, he finds it in the self-same Mrs. Hirsch. After all, as he himself has stated, albeit in unscientific language, she is a "lu-lu".

G.   THE OLD BLOCKS CAN CHIP

There can be no mistaking the power for good or ill that woman as wife and mother can have on her spouse and family. The further fact is that father as well as mother—and especially both together—can have a crucial influence on their progeny. Frank Gilroy, a brilliant young playwright, deals with this in a fine play.

"The Subject Was Roses"

Text: The fathers have eaten sour grapes,
           and the children's teeth are set on edge.
                                                    —Jeremiah 31:28

When the subject is roses, priceless literary lines may come to mind. One of these might be: "A rose is a rose is a rose" written by Gertrude Stein. Another might be that of the English bard who wrote: "A rose by any other name smells just as sweet".

Now, a young American playwright, Frank D. Gilroy, has written a play entitled "The Subject Was Roses". It is fair to say that none of his lines about the subject of roses will live in literary history as do Shakespeare's and Stein's. It is just as fair to add that Gilroy did not intend to produce anything that would earn a place among the timeless expressions about the beauty of this particular floral species.

All that he intended—and he succeeded admirably to fulfill his intention—was to write an excellent play about a family situation with its tragi-comic qualities. In the course of the play, as a kind of aid to bring the play to its climax, there figures a bouquet of roses. Such a floral gift is presented to the stage wife and mother, Nettie Cleary (played by Irene Dailey), by her husband, John (Jack Albertson) and son, Timmy (Martin Sheen).

The motivation for this show of affection, and what follows as a result of it, bring into focus the playwright's insights into the real-life situation of an unhappily-married couple who have an only son. The fact that the latter is presented as a newly returned veteran from the Second World War adds to the poignancy of the situation.

While Mr. Gilroy does not say anything memorable about roses, he does offer something very true and deep about how parents' relationships to each other affect their offspring. He makes more explicit what the Bible reports as a popular axiom of ancient days: "The fathers have eaten sour grapes, and the teeth of the children are set on edge."

H. COMMUNICATION—A FAILING ART

Causes for unhappy married life are several. An interesting and especially sad one is the lack of communication between husband and wife. Peter Shaffer has written meaningfully about this.

"The Private Ear" and "The Public Eye"

Text: And Rebekah lifted up her eyes, and when she saw
         Isaac, she lighted off the camel . . .
         And Isaac brought her into his mother Sarah's tent,
         and took Rebekah, and she became his wife; and he
         loved her . . .

                                          Genesis 24:64, 67

"The Private Ear" and "The Public Eye" are the titles of two one-act plays by the English dramatist, Peter Shaffer, which are being presented together at the Morosco Theatre.

Each play has its own story, independent of the other. It would be wrong, however, to imagine that they are unrelated to each other although they do tell different stories of an entirely different cast of characters.

The very titles of both plays suggest that they have their difference, along with a point in common. The ear and the eye are different parts of the body but they both have the quality of perception in common—one of hearing and the other of seeing.

In general, we may say that both plays deal with the common theme of communication with reference to love. "The Private Ear" tells of a young man who finds that his interest in beau-

tiful music, even romantic music, finds no reciprocal feeling
in the heart of the girl he would have fall in love with him,
as he would with her.

"The Public Eye", on the other hand, is the story of how
love can be established, or hopefully regained even without
words being spoken. Communication, not necessarily verbal, is
an essential for love. This is what Peter Shaffer is saying in both
plays.

The Biblical account of the meeting and marriage of Isaac
and Rebekah in the light of what we know of their subsequent
life together permits us to contemplate that their love for each
other was blessed with beautiful mutual understanding and
respect.

The Bible would agree with the truth of "The Private Ear"
and "The Public Eye" about love depending on communication. It would base this communication, however, ideally on a
man and woman's priceless soul.

I. CHOOSING A MATE
1. A Gamble

Granted that marriage has many drawbacks and dangers, it
still remains a fundamental social institution. No societal life
would be possible without it. Therefore, in spite of its weakness,
the institution must be maintained. A fine motion picture, produced in Hollywood, pointed out the gamble and uncertainties
of marriage.

"Love with the Proper Stranger"

Text: And on the seventh day God finished His work
       which He had made; and He rested on the seventh
       day from all His work which He had made.
                                    —Genesis 2:2

A delightful story is told of a young lady who declared herself
to be extremely nervous over her approaching marriage. Her
friends tried to encourage by pointing out to her that her own
parents had been married also. "O, that's different," she pro-
tested, "since in my parents' case, Mother married Daddy. In
my case, I am to marry a stranger!"

This story is appropos in thinking about the current motion picture, "Love with the Proper Stranger". The film tells of a musician (Steve McQueen) who following an accidental acquaintance with a young woman (Natalie Wood) finds that he and she face a serious situation together. How this situation is met and how love for each other finally comes to both of them are the subject of the movie.

The difficulties they encounter in the course of their leaving their status of strangers to that of being lovers seem to be more than ordinary human beings could cope with on their own resources. Indeed, that they should have met each other altogether was something which neither of them had planned. Thus it appears that a Power greater than themselves was involved with their lives and their love.

This brings to mind the interesting traditional answer dealing with the question as to what God has been doing since the time, as the Bible states, "God finished his work . . . and rested on the seventh day." The answer has it that God, upon finishing Creation, is engaged with mating couples. These couples, it should be noted, are always strangers, because incest is properly forbidden.

Considering all that is involved in mating strangers, it does require divine intercession. After all, what is desired is not only that the perfect strangers meet, but that their ensuing love be perfect, too. This surely is enough to keep God occupied eternally.

2. Not Easy

The difficulties with finding a proper mate begin early in life—even as early as adolescence. Indeed, it is this kind of searching and discovery which makes the period of adolescence in many ways far from a happy time. Nevertheless, this subject has been used as the theme for a popular play which also has been made into a movie.

"Come Blow Your Horn"

Text: The Song of Songs

The Biblical book, The Song of Songs, refers to the most

beautiful of songs, the song of love. This portion of the Scriptures is exceptional in its lyrical qualities, its use of poetry and language in general. It does not, however, tell a simple story, nor does it recite of a love that is untroubled.

Quite the contrary, the very meaning of the background of the recital, and the identification of the persons involved are subjects for speculation till this day. Whoever those involved may be, there is no mistaking the fact that the lovers were having difficulties.

This is not an unusual occurrence, for we know that true love hardly ever runs smoothly. Nevertheless, we may have to be reminded every once in a while of the pang of a young adult's growing up and finding his or her life's companion.

Recently on Broadway, and presently released as a film is a play entitled, "Come Blow Your Horn". It tells in a humorous fashion of the efforts of two brothers—first, the elder, then the younger—to go out on their own and sow their wild oats, before settling down. Their father grumpily complains of these shenanigans, while their mother, ever solicitous for her children's welfare, innocently busies herself in caring for their wants. Excellently acted, first by the Broadway cast, headed by Hal March, and now by the Hollywood troupe featuring Frank Sinatra, Joseph Stein's play furnishes much hilarity.

Through all the laughter, there must be recognized the seriousness of the period which is crucial in the lives of parents and their maturing children—the time of finding a mate. As in The Song of Songs, for all its beauty, it is not an easy time.

There is, however, this to be remembered. Somehow, in most cases, things work out quite well, and they "live happily ever after".

Interestingly, the family in "Come Blow Your Horn" is presented variously as Jewish or as Italian. It really makes no difference for the point of the story. It happens in all groups.

J. LOVE OR LONELINESS

Granted that marriage is fraught with uncertainties—thank God for His help—it still continues to be mankind's best answer not only for child rearing—but to meet the ever present problem of loneliness.

"The L-Shaped Room"

Text: And the Lord God said: It is not good
        that man should be alone.

—Genesis 2:18

Before Eve was long in this world, it may safely be assumed, the woman, made of the same flesh and spirit as Adam, had similar reactions to his. She knew as he the pang of loneliness and how it could be assuaged only by the love of and for another.

Adam and Eve, and every man, woman and child down through the ages to the present moment have equated loneliness with lovelessness. To be completely unloved and unloving is to be so incomplete a human personality as to find life worthless, even a living death.

Companionship and friendship can apply to people of the same sex. Love can be recognized between parents and children, and among members of a family unit. Since Adam and Eve, however, it is the love between man and woman that has been recognized as God's greatest boon to humanity in its effort to offset the evil of loneliness.

Love between the sexes being so central, sex itself has come to play a significant role in the human struggle against loneliness. Sometimes its expression is acceptable by society's standards. Sometimes it is considered anti-social and dishonorable.

A fascinating and original analysis of aspects of this situation is pictured in the British film, "The L-Shaped Room". The title at first suggests symbolically the loneliness, and the incompleteness of the life of the heroine, Leslie Caron, who is the occupant of such a room in an English rooming house. Her struggle against her loneliness, the beautiful and seamy side of her love, and that of her neighbors, are the subject of the movie.

By the end of the picture, Leslie Caron finds the room beautiful instead of ugly, for now in place of loneliness its L shape symbolizes for her the love she found there.

For every Adam and Eve, the truth is that loneliness can lose while love can regain something of Paradise.

K. LOVE AND LOYALTY GO TOGETHER

Since love plays such a central role in human experience, it is not surprising that much has been thought about it. Whatever may be said of love's essence and power, there can be no denying that true love implies loyalty. A French moving picture, which all in all is a spoof of a certain type of adventure story recently came to our shores with a very clear statement about this aspect of love.

"Cartouche"

Text: A woman of valor who can find?
       For her price is far above rubies . . .
       She doeth him good and no evil
       All the days of her life . . .
                                        —Proverbs 31:10, 12

Cartouche is the name of the character playing the title role of the enjoyable French film currently showing at the Lincoln Art Theatre in New York City. He is, however, less the hero of the movie bearing his name than Venus, his girl friend, is its heroine.

This is so because of the nature of the moving picture and of the essential characteristics expected of heroes and heroines.

The latter, whatever other qualities they may possess, are expected to be proponents of the good, and to be instruments for redemption where there is evil.

In the case of "Cartouche", we have a moving picture vehicle which spoofs swashbuckling exploits. The promotional blurb that is meant to encourage attendance informs that "foes fell by the score, and so did the ladies for that man among men, that rogue among rogues".

Presented as a kind of Robin Hood, robbing the rich and giving to the poor, Cartouche is a swashbuckling, heroic figure. The trouble is that he swashes so very much that his heroism buckles under the weight of improbability.

Venus, his lady friend, is far more believable as the heroine. Her Greek name bespeaks the beauty she possesses. It also suggests that she cannot be expected to be all that is associated with the ideal Hebrew woman as she is presented in the Book of Proverbs, Chapter Thirty-One.

For all of that, when at the end, Venus lies bedecked with precious jewelry, having given her life for her beloved, the line from Proverbs comes to mind: "A woman of valor . . . Her price is far above rubies".

This beautiful young lady had too much in her way of life to prevent her from asserting an "Amen" to the Biblical concept of an ideal woman. She was enough of a heroine, however, to affirm of the scriptural ideal of loyalty to one's beloved—C'est vrai! How true!

Preoccupation with Wealth

Make A Living, Get Rich— But Don't Lose Your Soul

The best part of an active man's waking day is usually devoted to earning a living, and if possible, to getting rich. In a sense, to this end of making money the education of children and young people is directed, and that of adults is similarly frequently aimed. It is money that more and more is regarded as the basis for achieving a desirable status in society. Money makes possible a fine home, country club affiliation, socializing with the "best people", fine food, clothes, expensive vacations, etc. Without money, runs the popular maxim, a man is no man.

Undoubtedly, money is power. It is a power, however, that can be a blessing or a curse. In the Great Society, a higher standard of living will be forthcoming; such a standard will necessarily mean higher income and greater wealth. There is, however, danger in this very improvement of the financial situation, even as there is cause for apprehension and concern where there is poverty. It is a danger to the moral and ethical values of living.

The material in this chapter is not a treatment of the economic theories of society—such as that of communism particularly, or of economic determinism generally, which maintain that everything in the human condition has an economic base and motivation. It does not deal with capitalism or socialism.

There have been and are a number of movies and plays dealing with these specific areas of modern society.

The contents of this chapter, however, present some evaluation in the light of the Bible of human behavior as involved in the making of money and the amassing of wealth.

A. MONEY, MONEY

1. Money Über Alles

So strong is the selfish desire in the human hearts for wealth that every other consideration, even the noblest tenets of civilized living, may be swept away when these stand in the way. Friedrich Duerrenmatt, the eminent playwright, gave a striking example of this in his splendid play which also has appeared in a movie version.

"The Visit"

Text: And if a man have committed a sin worthy of death,
and he be put to death, and thou hang him on a tree,
but thou shalt surely bury him the same day;
for he that is hanged is a reproach unto God . . .
                                   —Deuteronomy 21, 22, 23

The movie version of the play, "The Visit", the distinguished work of the Swiss playwright, Friedrich Duerrenmatt, differs somewhat from the play. In the latter which is the original, the character, Anton Schill, is put to death by order of a Court decision, because of an accusation against him. In the movie, he is given his life by the intercession of the very one who accused him.

The story in both versions is approximately the same, except for the difference in the endings. Anton, while a young man, had grievously wronged a young girl, who was driven from the town. Years later, she returns as a fabulously wealthy woman who offers to enrich the community on condition that Anton be punished for what he had done to her.

In both the play and the movie, we are shown how the thought of being materially enriched leads his fellow townsfolk to turn against Anton, even to the point of being willing to kill him for his youthful crime. It is not justice as such that leads to this judgment, but really ulterior motives of personal gain.

Indeed, the point is made in both versions of "The Visit" that where there is selfish profit involved, you will find that claims for human ideals are generally superseded. These may be cited as the reason for an action, but it is only a piece of hypocrisy.

In the play, the Burgomaster says: "In the name of humanity, we shall never accept" (the wronged woman's offer of riches for Anton's life). In the movie, the judge asks: "Have you anything to say in your defence before judgment is pronounced?" Anton answers: "I'm a human being."

In both cases, finally, the claims for consideration for a human being are unheeded, and the law of the Bible is broken.

Scripture teaches that the body of even a murderer—since it is that of a human being—must be treated with respect!

2. It's Maddening

This lust for gold when permitted to get out of control certainly can be most upsetting. It has the power to render one a madman.

"It's a Mad, Mad, Mad, Mad World"

Text: And it came to pass, that he saw the calf
        and the dancing, and Moses' anger waxed hot . . .
                                            —Exodus 32:19

Two negatives, may produce a positive. For example, if one says, "He was not unseen", it means: "He was seen".

Double negatives, however, do not always produce a positive, except as two no's may mean "no" positively. Thus a man may say: "No! No!" and mean thereby "No, definitely".

There is a current motion picture film that uses one adjective not only twice but four times consecutively in its title. The title is "It's A Mad, Mad, Mad, Mad World". This must be taken to mean that much of human life is mad, definitely, and how!

Intended as a comedy, its cast is replete with star comedians. These lend their humorous abilities to acting out the story which shuns the ludicrousness of human behavior. As the story has it, several people hear of a buried treasure and resolve to retrieve it. They try to hide from one another what their true intentions are in this regard. Their exploits, their chicaneries, and disappointments all add up to comic situations, confirming the title's claim.

All that the movie intends to do—and it fulfills its intention —is to show the humorousness of people's avidity for money. One cannot help but think, however, that there is something very serious about this tendency.

The Bible recalls the incident of idolatrous worship of a Golden Calf. This idol has become symbolic of man's lust for wealth. There is surely grave damage in such idolatry both for society and for man's own happiness and peace of mind.

This inordinate zeal for gold makes it a "mad, mad, mad, mad world". Madness in one sense means something ludicrous, and therefore funny. It also means insane, and therefore something very serious.

3. A Driving Force

What has become a classic example of the driving force impelling a success-bent individual who has made his financial success his supreme and only value in life, has been provided by the well-known author, Budd Schulberg.

"What Makes Sammy Run?"

Text: Thou shalt love thy neighbor as thyself.

—Leviticus 19:18

Some years ago, Budd Schulberg wrote the novel, "What Makes Sammy Run?" Now the novel has been converted into a smash hit musical comedy on Broadway.

The story-line is the same in the play as it was in the novel. As the plot unfolds, the question of what prompts Sammy Glick to behave as he does is not difficult to answer. Sammy as he rises from a newspaper copy boy to a Hollywood producer is interested in achieving worldly success as quickly and as largely as he can. To do this, he must be an eager beaver.

To change the analogy somewhat in order to make the point clearer, Sammy considers himself and others as being in a rat race. In such a situation, he reasons that success comes to the rattiest as well as to the swiftest.

This then is what makes Sammy run—a livid desire to make his mark in a world which, according to him, recognizes only material success. In so running, he steps on people, and makes them foot-stones on which to raise himself. Also, in his mad, mad haste to reach the top, he does not observe the lines of propriety and decency.

In all that Sammy does we may see a denial of the Biblical injunction to regard each man as one's brother whom it is proper to love.

Here is what may be said to be the crime of and punishment for Sammy's "running". The sin? He is unconscionable in his efforts to achieve three F's—Fame, Fun and Fortune. The punishment? He is doomed, therefore, to lose two F's—Family and Friends.

One of the characters in the play says to Sammy—and in this statement we have the end of the matter for all selfishness—"You can't eat your brothers and have them."

4.   The High Cost of Getting Rich

a.   A Cattleman

The bitter lesson to be learned from the life of the notorious Sammy Glick of "What Makes Sammy Run?" is one which has been presented frequently on stage and screen. The fundamental point is that wealth achieved at any cost—may prove to be acquired at too high a price. An illustration of this has been provided by a fictional cattleman.

"Hud"

> Text: Now Adonijah the son of Haggith exalted himself, saying: "I will be king . . ." And his father hath not grieved him all his life in saying "Why hast thou done so?"
>
>   —I Kings 1:5, 6

"Hud" is a strange, unfamiliar name. Its main claim to recognition lies in the fact that it belongs to the central figure of a novel which has been made into a current Academy Award winning picture. This fictional personality, besides having an odd name, has a character to match.

Unlike his name, however, this odd-ball, off-beat individual has frequently come into the ken of all of us. Frequently we have come across characteristics like his, although rarely in such a large measure as in Hud's case. His is the way of the unprincipled, selfish wise-guy.

As Hud's story unfolds, we witness ever more of his grasping, "devil-take-the-hindmost," "never-give-a-sucker-an-even-break," "I'm number one in the world" attitude and actions. In viciousness and immorality, he would take advantage of anyone and everyone—his own father, nephew, housekeeper and strangers-at-large.

Hud's father bears the burden of his somewhat good-looking son, rarely trying to curb him. In this we are reminded of King David and his son, Adonijah. The Bible tells that the latter, also "of beauteous appearance" vexed his father who did not chide him.

In the Bible, Adonijah is reported to have sought to rebel against his father while the King was on his death-bed. In our modern-day story, Hud is pictured as being of a like disposition concerning his ailing father.

Adonijah, we know, was unsuccessful in his attempt to wrest the kingship for himself. In Hud's case we are not told what finally happens to him, yet we can guess. Whatever he may be able to secure for himself of material things in the world, Hud is bound to receive the punishment of all selfishness. He is doomed to be a completely lonely man.

b. A Television Writer

Part of the payment for getting ahead through an unconscionable exploitation of others is the loss of popularity. Another loss—which is paid at the very outset—is a poisoned system of values which pictures all people as similarly rapacious. This idea has been explored in a Broadway play starring Robert Preston.

"Nobody Loves an Albatross"

Text: I trusted even when I spoke:
        "I am greatly afflicted."
        I said in my haste:
        "All men are liars."

                                        —Psalms 116:10, 11

That the title of the current Broadway hit play, "Nobody
Loves An Albatross" is strange should be quickly apparent.
Evidently, when Ronald Alexander, the author, gave the play
this unusual title, he must have wanted to draw attention to
some main ideas of the play.

Surprisingly, all of the New York drama critics failed to refer
to the meaning of the title in their reviews. Just as remarkable
is the fact that no mention of an albatross is made in the play.

What, then, could be the possible reason for such a title? The
play tells of a television writer and producer, charmingly played
by Robert Preston, who is a "phoney". He himself is aware of
this, and makes the most of it. Believing that all people are
phonies, he just tries to beat them at their own game.

Not creative, or capable of good writing, he makes use of
other writers more gifted than he. Claiming their work as his
own, he exploits them.

This television writer was always hanging around the necks
of others, much as that albatross, featured in "The Ancient
Mariner", was pictured as hanging around the neck of that
worthy sailor. For this very good reason, both he and the albatross were soundly disliked.

This explains the title, in part. Some individuals, like the
notorious albatross, may be real pains in the neck, but does this
mean that nobody is to be trusted? What would the Bible say
of the idea that all men are untrustworthy?

While the Psalmist indeed said, "All men are liars," he ad-
mitted that he was rendering a snap judgment. The Psalmist
declared unmistakably that his fundamental faith remained in
man's trustworthiness.

"Nobody Loves an Albatross", as a title, brings to mind that
some men do take advantage of others. This phrase has nothing
to do, however, with the play's main idea that all men are

untrustworthy. Could it be that our author used a catchy title in order to entice an audience? Even granted that this be so, it still would not prove his own point that all men are phoney, and that an albatross is their symbol.

B. THE ORGANIZATION MAN

It has been recognized for a long time that in the getting of money man is in danger of losing his soul. This does not mean that wealth necessarily means wickedness, but it does mean that the glitter of gold has in it a special ability to blind a man to the true values of life.

Lately a new danger has been added to the dignity of man as he seeks to make a living. Huge business corporations, in order to earn the greatest profit along with achieving utmost efficiency, have instituted systems and regimens of conduct which can rob their employees of their individuality. A timely play— a comedy at that—has pointed up this situation.

"The Absence of a Cello"

Text: I am the Lord, thy God, who brought thee out of Egypt, out of the house of bondage.
—Exodus 20:2

Every period in history develops some particular identity. This distinguishing characteristic is frequently conveyed through some new and distinct term or phrase. In the First World War, the word "doughboy" made its appearance, and it told of millions of soldiers. The Second World War produced the term, G.I., and it meant millions of American servicemen.

In our day, the phrases "jet-age", "A.O.K.", "rock-and-roll" are a few examples of the type of living which is contemporaneous. Others with which we are familiar are "the man in the grey flannel suit", "the organization man" and "conformity". These latter terms may deal with economic phases of a person's life but they actually describe much more. Just how widespread and deep is their influence is suggested in a current Broadway comedy hit—"The Absence of a Cello".

The play tells of a world-renowned physics professor who because of money problems is seeking employment with a large business firm. He is advised that this modern corporation, as all others like it, will engage only a certain type of individual who fits the company's concept of a wholesome personality. Such things as dress, the type of automobile to be driven, the people with whom to socialize, the books to read, are a few of the matters on which the company has a fixed standard for acceptance. The scientist is advised that the cello which he plays should be hidden away when the company investigator visits his home for the interview. A cello, it is claimed, might indicate a personality which is too introspective for the company's acceptable personnel.

What is shown here in humorous fashion is the serious side of modern society's demand for conformity from the restricted organization man.

The Bible which holds forth Freedom as a luminous virtue must have strong objection to this kind of benighted slavishness. In Holy Writ, the symbolic enforced absence of a cello might well be written down as a real loss of soul.

C. AUTOMATION

Added to the evil implied in the concept of an "organization man" there is in modern big business and industry with its ever increasing mechanization, another new threat to men and women known as "automation". As automation becomes the hall-mark of modern business and industry, unemployment and a loss of human dignity and worth of the worker and laborer come to the fore. It is to be expected that today's topical reviews should deal with this great issue.

"The Committee"

Text: I remember for thee the affection of thy youth . . .
How thou wentest after me in the wilderness . . .
—Jeremiah 2:2

"The Committee" is the name of a group of young talented actors who produce and enact topical reviews. Originating from

San Francisco's North Beach in what was once a funeral parlor, they have appeared in New York with an unusually lively set of skits.

These short presentations are meant to entertain and also to offer comment, often unspoken, but always pertinent, on our present-day weaknesses and foibles.

One of the most successful and meaningful of these is a scene featuring an automaton and a beggar. The robot, dressed like a man, moves mechanically back and forth on the stage while the beggar keeps asking it or him (?) for a dime.

Every once in a while the robot tips his hat. The beggar takes this to be a sign of recognition and encouragement. Soon the needy man realizes that there is no real response from the machine. All that he gets is an empty gesture.

Only when the beggar begins to remonstrate with the machine does the mechanical man forsake his methodical unconcern. Then, he lifts his cane and beats the unfortunate beggar mercilessly and thoroughly.

Here in this short skit is portrayed so much of the tragic evil lurking in our day of automation. The machine has become almost man enough to appear to respond to human need. On the other hand, man has taken on so much of the character of the machine age, that he has lost his human empathy.

What is needed so very much in the midst of modern automation is an unremitting effort on the part of modern society not to lose the basic sentiments which emphasize the dignity and worth of every man. This was the ideal of the early, simple societies.

It is to this human ideal that the prophet called his contemporaries when he spoke of God's love for Israel when they followed Him in the wilderness. The same call sounds even more urgently today.

D. BUSINESS ETHICS

It must be obvious that even in the most recent development of man's industrial and financial interests the ancient Biblical spirit of love of neighbor remains a fundamental principle.

Certainly, the Bible's teachings of honesty and justice are not
outdated. A play by Joseph Hayes dealing with modern business methods illustrates this excellently.

"Calculated Risk"

Text: The vineyard of Naboth.

—I Kings 21:1–24

The story of Naboth's vineyard is one of intrigue, perjury
and crooked dealing. King Ahab (ca. 850 B.C.E.) desired to
possess a vineyard that belonged to a certain Naboth.
The latter refused to part with it for any consideration, because it was his family heritage. According to the ancient customs of Israel, Naboth was completely within his rights in
refusing to sell or to relinquish his possession to the king. There
was nothing that Ahab could do about it.

Jezebel, who was Ahab's queen, determined that the king
would secure that vineyard nevertheless. To accomplish her
purpose she bribed two witnesses who testified falsely that Naboth had blasphemed God and king. For this alleged crime,
Naboth was put to death. His vineyard was then confiscated by
the Crown.

This story has a contemporaneous ring. We all know of instances where trumped up charges pervert justice. We are familiar—only too well—with the chicanery that robs the innocent
of their possessions and their rights. A play currently showing
on Broadway, "Calculated Risk" deals with the crooked manipu-
lations that can take place in a modern business enterprise.
Starring Joseph Cotten, and presented as a who-done-it mystery,
the drama deals with the same human failings that were those
of Ahab and Jezebel.

Another point of similarity between the Biblical account of
Naboth's vineyard and the play written by Joseph Hayes is the
style of the writing. Since Henrik Ibsen featured the so-called
modern drama, it has been maintained that straightforward,
simple language is its hall-mark. "Calculated Risk" is written
precisely in such a style. I Kings is also distinguished for its
simple prose.

This similarity of style can lead to the proper conclusion that

there is much of modern Broadway in the ancient Bible. It is
even more correct to say that there is much of the ancient Bible
on today's Broadway.

E. AVOIDING PITFALLS ON
THE PATH OF ETHICAL SUCCESS

The warnings expressed in many of today's plays about the
pitfalls on the path of success are not really new. They represent
a good deal of the wisdom and tested truth of the Bible. Thus,
even a play dealing with so modern a person as a Hollywood
actor can call attention to the fundamental truth that making
a living has something to do with making a life.

"Will Success Spoil Rock Hunter?"

Text: And Satan stood up against Israel,
        and moved David to number Israel.
                                    —I Chronicles 21:1

The figure of Satan appears in different guises in Scriptures.
In one instance, he entices King David to commit the wrong
of taking a census of the people, an act which was forbidden in
those days. For this the Bible reports that the king and the nation was made to suffer.

Here the Holy Book presents Satan as both a troubler and an
enticer. The Adversary of Israel appealed to King David's vanity
in encouraging the monarch to number the people. Satan understood the King's natural desire to glory in his power and success.

A fascinating and funny play, "Will Success Spoil Rock
Hunter?" by George Axelrod (recently produced at the Bergen
Mall Playhouse) may be said to present a modern version of
similar satanic endeavor. The author pictures a fictional literary
agent, Irving La Salle, as a kind of Satan, who at a fee of part
of his client's soul satisfies the desires of a writer, George Mac-
Cauley, for "success".

As the plot unfolds, George gets into the spirit of Hollywood
and its peculiar social values, generally regarded as glamorous.
In the process, he forfeits more and more of his soul to his
agent who aids him to achieve success a la Hollywood.

It so happens that George in his earlier days of innocence had written a magazine article concerning a movie star, entitling it, "Will Success Spoil Rock Hunter?" What finally happens to George gives the audience an idea of a probable answer to the question raised about Rock. You see, it all depends. It depends on whether Rock, or George, or anyone who travels the path of "success", stumbles and falls. Additionally, it depends on whether he remains conscious or becomes oblivious to the fact that he is falling.

F. AN UN-HERO

In spite of everything we believe, it is interesting to observe how the thought that success—in the sense of loads of money—should be acquired, even if necessary by dubious means, still holds a popular appeal for many. The public applauded such a display of "smart operation" by the charming, un-heroic hero of a smash musical comedy.

"How to Succeed in Business
Without Really Trying"

Text: My son, keep my words,
        And lay up my commandments with thee.
                                                        —Proverbs 7:1
        Say unto wisdom, "Thou art my sister",
        And call understanding thy kinswoman;
        That they may keep thee from the strange woman,
        From the alien woman that maketh smooth her words.
                                                        —ibid. 7:4, 5

The present Broadway hit, "How to Succeed in Business Without Really Trying" has won many awards as an outstanding musical comedy. One can be certain that the play's success has been achieved precisely because it did not carry out its own theme. Everyone connected with the production—its authors, musical composer, actors et al—has exerted his or her best efforts for the resulting awards and acclaim.

What is the prescription for success dealt with in the play? It is that in the modern business world the old idea that one should work hard and honestly in order to achieve promotion and advancement no longer is true. Today, a young man needs only to play up to the powers-that-be and cater to their personal idiosyncrasies and foibles, and he can go very far, even to the top.

In the course of presenting an example of how this formula is presumed to work out, the play affords a good many laughs for the audience.

Laughs aside, though, how does the play's proposition appear in the light of the Bible? Scriptures maintain that sound ethics are basic to all endeavors in life—the raising of a family, the practicing of a profession, the running of a business, etc.

Furthermore, a man's character is a reflection of how he conducts himself in the various aspects of his life, including, of course, his business dealings.

The Book of Proverbs is a compendium of practical wisdom. It would understand why "How to Succeed" would win awards as a musical comedy. It would, however, reserve the highest award—that for successful living—to a different type of hero.

G.   CLASS TELLS—WHAT?

It would be a mistake to conclude that people generally accept the notion that success is its own validation. Along with the Bible, most men and women, being decent people, have faith that success is not only undesirable without good character, but that such proper qualities of character are what will insure success. An Academy Award winning film furnishes an example of this faith.

"The Hustler"

Text: Thus saith the Lord:
        "Let not the wise man glory in his wisdom,
        Neither let the mighty man glory in his might,
        Let not the rich man glory in his riches;
        But let him that glorieth glory in this,
        That he understandeth, and knoweth Me."
                                        —Jeremiah 9:22

How come that Eddie, a gifted pool shark, has lost to Minnesota Fats, a bigger but slightly less able pool player? This is the question raised in the Academy Award winning film, "The Hustler".

It is left for a gambler in the picture to explain that Eddie, it is true, had talent, more talent than Fats, but he lacked the qualities of character necessary for victory. In the course of their match Eddie had taken to the bottle, and as result became drunk. "Talent is not character," says the gambler to Eddie, "and without character, you are bound to lose."

This idea that good character is necessary for victory in sports was being discussed widely not so long ago. Leo Durocher, who later said that he had been misquoted, was understood to have said: "Nice guys never finish first."

This matter of character with reference to sports victory is frankly not as important as the larger and more significant subject of good character and its necessity for victory in the Game of Life.

Long ago, the Prophet Jeremiah declared his faith that talent, wealth, wisdom are all insufficient to insure real, abiding success or victory. What is needed is a knowledge of the Lord, said the Prophet.

Although it frequently happens that sharpies, and muscle men and wise guys and those who bribe seem to succeed, their success is only apparent, and never lasting. Most often they fail without even the seeming victory.

The Prophet in his own way had expressed the truth that hustling must lead to nowhere unless the hustler (used here in good sense) is possessed of good character.

III

Learning to Live

Educate, Educate, Educate

Only Man among the creatures of the Earth can know the meaning of education. The beasts, fowl, fish, insects and other creeping things may be trained, but none of them can be educated. Education is a uniquely human experience and differential. As such, it must occupy a central position in any full discussion of the nature of Man. The simple truth is that there is no truly human being without education. An ignorant man is less a man than one who is educated. The loss of a man's humanity may be seen to be in direct proportion to his ignorance.

This does not mean that all education is necessarily a blessing. There are too many cases in history where whole peoples have been educated—actually indoctrinated—with wrong instruction as to the way to go. Such wrong education with its frightful results prompts many who take life seriously to think long and hard about proper education and to offer the results of their philosophizing to society. Among these thinkers one finds concern with such matters as the proper content of, and the correct psychological approaches for successful learning.

Since education is so vital a matter for each individual, for society and for the future of mankind in general, it is not surprising that the greatest minds have turned to its consideration in every generation. It should be no cause for wonderment, either, that the Bible offers most penetrating insights into this area of human experience, and that the contemporary theatre reflects many aspects of the educational situation of modern man.

The material in this chapter, selected from the Bible and today's theatre, is for the purpose of presenting first, some educational thoughts about "Modern Youth" (A), second, some statements about "The Teaching of Morality" (B), and finally,

some suggestions, "Proper Perspectives", as to how to realize
the Bible's values in modern society (C).

A. THE YOUTH OF TODAY

1. Better or Worse? That Is a Question

Education is meant to be a lifelong occupation. In ancient
times the learned scholar, most highly respected, was never a
callow youth. In modern times—except for a most recent emphasis on "adult education"—it has been generally felt that
schooling was for children and for young people. While insist-
ing that education is meant for all ages, no one can deny the
importance of education of the young—especially when we think
of education as more than just a matter of simply attending
school. More especially still, is the importance of proper education of young people borne in upon us when we consider how
today's youth—the hope of the future—may be variously evaluated. This matter comes to the fore in many a motion picture,
particularly one which shows most disquieting scenes of modern
youth.

"Malamondo"

Text: These are the generations of Jacob;
        Joseph being seventeen years old,
        was feeding the flock with his brethren,
        being still a lad . . .
        and Joseph brought evil report of them unto their
        father.
                                              —Genesis 37:2

A burning question of the hour is: "From a moral point of
view, are today's young people as good as in past generations
or are they worse?" Some argue strongly that they are indeed
much worse. Others maintain just as vociferously that there have
never been finer youths than ours.
    This question is raised in its stark drama in a current motion
picture, entitled significantly, "Malamondo". Meaning "evil
world", the picture shows how the young people of several

nations are living in a very "sick world". Indeed, life for them is so "sick" that quite a number of them—especially in Sweden and Norway, according to statistics—are seeking death through suicide. Ministers of religion there, according to "Malamondo", have the duty not only to save souls, but actually to save lives.

Does this not mean that our young generation is worse morally and spiritually than any previous one? Before hastening to answer in the affirmative, let us bear in mind the many splendid achievements of young people in building a better world. So much of this is performed unselfishly as in the Peace Corps.

All that we can say on the basis of "Malamondo" is that there are in extreme camps of young people some who are destroying as well as are being destroyed spiritually. Certainly one of the reasons for this is recognized biblically as being in the very nature of youth.

The word in Hebrew for youth is "Naar", the root of which means restlessness, uprootedness. From Joseph's time till today's teenager, it is true that adolescence and youth are a difficult time for adjustment. In this sense there is extra meaning to the witticism attributed to George Bernard Shaw: "Youth is such a wonderful thing. What a crime it is to waste it on children."

2. Growing Should Be Up

Considering the state of modern civilization, and the volatile and changing nature of youth, the need for proper educational goals has become immensely urgent. Always education must aim to help young people develop into wholesome and mature adults. Maturation must mean "growing up", not only physically but mentally and emotionally as well. According to one motion picture which we may use as an example of several contemporary pictures and plays dealing with the same theme, today's world has too many "babies" who are the parents of little ones.

"The Pumpkin Eater"

Text: Therefore thus saith the Lord God:
        "Because thou hast forgotten Me,
        and cast Me behind thy back, therefore
        bear also thy lewdness and thy harlotries."
                                        —Ezekiel 23:35

Currently there is being shown a movie based on a novel, both of which are entitled "The Pumpkin Eater"—that derives its name from a popular nursery rhyme. The rhyme is about Peter, the pumpkin eater, who "had a wife and couldn't keep her; he put her in a pumpkin shell and there he kept her very well". The striking thing about this dramatic production is that while this has a title which stems from children's lore, it is best described as "adult entertainment".

As we all know, any play or movie is said to be for "adults only", when the vehicle deals with some aspect of immorality in a way which is too harsh and raw for young ears and minds.

Granted the reasonableness of such procedure, it is very interesting to observe that the very title, "The Pumpkin Eater", seems to suggest a great truth about the immoralities presented in "adult entertainment". Very frequently, they reflect immature people who never grow up properly.

Such immorality is writ large in almost every scene of "The Pumpkin Eater" dealing with the marital difficulties and infidelities, not only of the main characters but of their entire circle, and indeed of society itself. Not all of the trouble may be attributed to a lack of maturity, but it does play a significant role. What is needed obviously, is a more mature attitude to life and its sacred values.

In "The Pumpkin Eater", a religion revivalist appears at the door of the unfortunate heroine, declaring that Ezekiel already in Bible times warned against the kind of evil that has taken hold of modern society. She gives him some money for one of his projects, saying, "Maybe this will help me."

Perhaps it is because the title of the film speaks of a pumpkin, that his appearance and her giving him support for his proposed radio station in Jerusalem, has the quality of a trick or treat routine. This kind of "religious" response is as immature as Halloween, and just as ineffectual.

3. Education Is Life

It has been known for a long time that "school-learning", or "book-knowledge" is not quite the same as "education from life". Fortunately, life has the ability to educate those who are willing to learn from it. The success of many of man's strivings depends upon his utilization of life's experiences. This facet of the ongoing education process of living may be observed in a charming play dealing with the situation of a young coed, her parents, and her fiance.

"Take Her, She's Mine"

Text: The crown of the elders is their progeny,
        And the glory of the children is their parents.
                                                —Proverbs 17:6

One of the tests for human happiness is the nature of the parent-child relationship. The Book of Proverbs describes the ideal in this regard. It declares the hoped for situation as one where the parents and the child have reason to be proud of and be happy with each other.

Because by definition and nature, the parents represent the "old" generation and the child the "new", there are perforce differences which may strain the reasons for mutual esteem and pride. In addition, education, especially in the form of the present-day college experience which is meant by the parents to be a tool to help them derive more satisfaction from their collegiate children, may frequently emphasize the differences. Inexperienced, and seeking the facts of life, crammed with book knowledge, but devoid of the real facts of living, the youngsters on campus desperately need understanding and guidance. So, also, do the parents who frequently are "disappointed" with the results of a college education for their children.

There are both unfortunate and fortunate sides to this thing. Unfortunately, the need for patience and understanding is often not recognized by either or both parents and children. Fortunately, there is an on-going maturation process which helps straighten matters.

In an hilarious manner, "Take Her, She's Mine", the recent Broadway play which now has been making the rounds of New York suburban theatres, such as our neighborhood Bergen Mall Playhouse, deals with this "infernal" triangle of college, parents and students.

Without giving away too much of the solution to the problem, we may say that the play suggests that "Take Her, She's Mine" must become "take her, she's yours".

4. Love May Not Come Naturally

Because life can be regarded as educative, a repeated warning must be issued against imagining that just by living one grows naturally wise. An extremely popular case can be made for "doing what comes naturally" in many of life's situations. One must be on guard, however, against believing that our deepest and fondest yearnings can be achieved "naturally". A motion picture which has won fame for its delightful, child-like charm must be seen to be just that—childish in one of its basic propositions.

"Lilli"

Text: To everything there is a season,
        and a time to every purpose under the heaven.
                                    —Ecclesiastes 3:1

"Lilli" is not just any girl's name anymore. Since Leslie Caron bore that name as she enacted the title role of the moving picture, "Lilli" has come to mean something special.

It has come to remind movie-goers of a simply charming and charmingly simple motion picture. It has come also to remind playgoers of the long-running Broadway musical comedy, "Carnival", which was based on Lilli's story.

This Lilli was scarcely sixteen years of age when she was orphaned. She set out to find employment in one of her native French towns. Being young, innocent and starry-eyed, she might have fallen victim to those ready to take advantage of her.

At a carnival where she was saved from committing suicide by a puppeteer, she secured a job with him. Her task was to engage in conversation with the puppets. As time went on, she learned to love not only the toy puppets, but also the man who operated them and whose expressions they were.

The puppeteer, Paul, also had to come to recognize his true love for her. It was Lilli then who spoke the lines which are reminiscent of, although not the same as those of the Bible's Wisdom Literature. She said:

"There is a time for everything . . .
There is a time to lose one's parents . . .
There is a time to love . . ."

Up to this point she was quite in keeping with Holy Writ. She said further, however: "One does not learn these things. One just grows into them."

This additional comment about just naturally coming to know without needing to learn the meaning of love is contrary to what the Bible knew about life and love.

Let us not be too harsh with Lilli, though. After all, by the end of the film she was still a very young lady. Who should expect from her the Wisdom of Solomon?

5. Aging Means Changing

Surely, as we grow older, we change. How to recognize and deal with this aging process is a matter of direct concern for everyone. An interesting statement has been made in a little-known play about this well-known matter.

"Just for Tonight"

Text: And Abraham was old, advanced in age.
                                                —Genesis 24:1

One of the basic principles of a certain school of Biblical exegesis is that not a word or even letter in the Scriptures is superfluous. These Biblical expositors claim that what may appear redundant is really not so at all. It is there to teach a message of the spirit.

The following is an example of this type of commentary . . . "Having said that Abraham was 'old' (Gen. 24:1), why does the text repeat the idea, saying that the patriarch was 'advanced in age'? It is in order to teach that as Abraham grew older, he advanced, i.e. became an ever better human being."

Such an interpretation highlights the special merit of Abraham. Unlike so many men and women who do not improve in character as they grow older, Abraham did.

This explanation also points to the implied truth that aging must bring changes not only physically but also spiritually to every human being. A recognition of this truth is necessary for an adjustment to life.

Recently at the Bergen Mall Playhouse, Gloria Swanson was featured in a satisfying play, "Just For Tonight" which dealt with this theme. Playing the role of a former Hollywood queen, Miss Swanson returns to her hometown. There she hopes to pick up again strands of her life she had dropped in her youth. She wants to make real the poetic wish:

> Time, fly backward
> Make me a child again
> Only for tonight.

By the close of the play its author reminds the audience through his heroine that no one can revise the course of time and live the youthful life of years gone by. Miss Swanson affirms the truth that former love songs can only be sung as memories, once a swan song has been part of one's repertoire.

B. MORALS ARE TAUGHT

1. Learn War No More

The success of an individual and of society as a whole in achieving the dual goal of survival and happiness obviously depends to a great extent on education. What we have to learn is that happiness may be variously conceived but in no case can it be meaningful unless it does not deny moral principles. Also man's survival can not be predicated on immorality.

In our modern world, the happiness and survival of men, women and children are seriously threatened by the Third World War which could mean the end of civilization. What is desperately needed worldwide is an education of man's mind on how to see war as far from glorious, and as so despicable, in fact, as to be unthinkable.

"Oh, What a Lovely War"

Text: Nation shall not lift up sword against nation,
        nor shall they learn war any more.

                                            —Isaiah 2:4

By definition, satire is a literary manner which blends a critical attitude with humour and wit to the end that human institutions or humanity may be improved. By execution, "Oh, What a Lovely War", a British import to the Broadway stage, presents a satirical treatment of World War I in a rousing musical entertainment form.

The bitterness of the satire is expressed at once, along with its humorous quality, when the audience is made sensitive to the term, "war games". That the deploying of troops, the exploding of ammunition, the planning of strategy to annihilate the opposition should be called "a game" and especially, "a war game", points up the kind of peculiar situation in which mankind found itself just before 1914.

When the "war games" in preparation of World War I became converted into the real thing, "Oh, What a Lovely War", describing the developments, finds a natural satirical condition in the ludicrousness as well as the evil of so much that took place in the circles of the High Commands to the lowest levels on both sides.

Humorous bits, clever choreography, appropriate parodies, are some of the meaningful material. It all builds in the audience the appreciation of how wrong was so much of the reasons for and the results of the "war to end all war".

"Oh, What a Lovely War" produces the effect of all good satire, a criticism leading to a determination to set right what is wrong in society. A good way to begin in this regard is to do away with the whole procedure known as "war games".

Long ago, Isaiah expressed this hoped for situation, when he called for nations not only not to fight, but also not to learn war any more. There is nothing lovely about war—just as there is no loveliness in senseless suffering, or beauty in bestiality.

2 a.   Unlearn Insanity

One of the confounding difficulties in the way to removing war from the face of the globe is the fact that, strangely enough, war—this most immoral thing—appeals to the highest motives of man to practice it. Unconscionable in itself, war appeals to the conscience of man, calling for courage, sacrifice, loyalty, patri-

otism, etc. This produces a crazy situation indeed! Can man
unlearn this piece of insanity?

This question is raised indirectly and from two different
points of view in two fine motion pictures which won awards
for excellence. These pictures deserve to win the hearts of mankind.

"Bridge on the River Kwai"

Text: Who is blind but My servant?
Or deaf as My messenger that I send?
Who is blind as he that is whole-hearted,
And blind as the Lord's servant?

—Isaiah 42:19

"Madness!" With this one word the uniformed man with the
Red Cross armband expresses his impression of the events and
personalities figuring in "The Bridge on the River Kwai", a
most distinguished motion picture now enjoying a re-release.

Because of his role as a member of the Medical Corps, or as
a Red Cross worker, we may regard his opinion as that of a
humane person. Moreover, we may pay special attention to his
one-word reaction to the happenings at the Bridge, because
they approximate the human condition in general.

The story tells of a group of British soldiers, prisoners of
the Japanese in the Second World War, who are commanded
to build a bridge over the River Kwai, somewhere in South
Asia. The Japanese commander is cruel and vindictive in his
treatment of the prisoners. The British Colonel withstands this
cruelty in his insistence upon his rights and privileges as a
soldier. When he believes that his rights and those of his fellow
Britishers are recognized, then he directs his group to build
the best bridge possible as a sign of their duty and pride as
British soldiers.

When the bridge is about completed, a team of English com-
mandos appear to destroy it.

In the carnage that ensues, the opinion is voiced that all that
transpired in the building of the bridge was nonsensical.

To confirm this reaction, one need only consider that so often
in life people suffer a kind of megalomania in their efforts to

achieve their purposes. Frequently these goals are pointless and fruitless, yet blind and almost insane devotion is given to their accomplishment.

Long ago, in referring not only to the business of soldiering and welfare, but to many of the aspects of living in general, the prophet Isaiah exclaimed: "Hear ye deaf, and look ye blind that ye may see . . . Who is blind as he that is whole-hearted?" The prophet recognized that sincerity in achieving a wrong, a meaningless goal, paves the way of human ridiculousness. All the needless pain, suffering and sacrifice and even heroics at the River Kwai point up the similar futile and insane pattern of much of society's way. In a word, so much of our life viewed from the aspect of humaneness is just plain——madness.

2 b. Unlearn Insanity—Improper Goals

Another motion picture, "The Great Escape", which deals with patriotic loyalty and sacrifice in time of war—obviously qualities to be praised—nevertheless raises the same question: Can man be free from the madness of war?

"The Great Escape"

Text: So Joshua arose, and all the people of war . . .
and Joshua chose out thirty thousand men of valour.
—Joshua 8:3

The waging of war calls for valor, especially by those who are doing the actual fighting. To be a man of war means to be courageous. The cowardly soldier is a contradiction in terms. That this is so is universally recognized.

There is also the generally accepted notion abroad that warfare is uniquely a great adventure. To face its dangers, to fight for life is to engage most frequently not only in individual acts of heroism, but also to join in actions with comrades-in-arms whose heroic hearts beat together in a way that is inspiring and quickening to the human spirit.

A current motion picture, "The Great Escape", which recounts a real World War II experience corroborates the usual impression of the engaging in war as a great adventure. It is an account of how seventy-six Allied fighters tried to escape from a German prison camp during the last Great War. Careful and clever plotting, amazing fortitude, cooperation that was wonderous, whole-hearted devotion to the cause, and valor on an immense scale—all went into the operation.

All of this, however, was spent in an effort that ended with fifty of the escapees killed, a number of them caught, and very few making good this escape.

One of the characters in this picture asks another: "Was it worth the cost?" Whatever the answer given in this film, I must say that the movie re-impressed me with the terrible waste caused by war.

If only the courage, resolution and skill spent in war would be dedicated in peace for a better world, what a finer world we would have!

3. All the World Loves a Baby

If learning is difficult, unlearning is at least doubly so. If learning what is sensible is hard, unlearning what is nonsensical, but deeply imbedded, is well nigh impossible. Mankind's future, however, depends on our ability to do precisely this—to rid civilization of its deeply ingrained prejudice, ignorance and insanity. For this, every means of education should be employed; every proper motivation should be used. Maybe—only maybe—an appeal to mankind to right itself for the sake of its beloved children, may win the day. Bob Hope, the famous humorist, in a recent film, said as much.

"A Global Affair"

Text: And the wolf shall dwell with the lamb,
And the leopard shall lie down with the kid, . . .
And a little child shall lead them.
—Isaiah 11:2

A bachelor is leading a gay life. Suddenly, and innocently, his life is complicated by a foundling baby which has been placed in his charge. His methods of dealing with the infant are inexperienced, although frequently ingenious, and always funny.

The presence of the child in his bachelor apartment leads to suspicion, and an effort to suppress the fact. All this affects his relationships with his girl friends as well as his associates at his place of business, and in general, throws his life into a dither. This has been the plot of a number of movies, which were intended to be comedies. With Bop Hope cast as the bachelor in the film, "A Global Affair", with just such a theme, the comedy may be expected to shine forth with special brilliance,

Add the United Nations Organization as the film's background—the bachelor is one of its minor officials, while the baby was found in the U.N. building—and the movie is given increased opportunities for mirth. For example, his girl friends from the U.N., who each offers her services to the bachelor to care for "his" baby hail from different countries, with consequent differences in customs and mores.

It is precisely this U.N. background, moreover, which gives the movie the fine proposition that the world's problems should be solved by bearing the world's children in mind. These little ones should be the universal concern of all people—regardless of national barriers, for these babies are free from national prejudices, and hatreds, and should be seen for what they are—dependent, tiny human beings. Since everyone loves a baby, "A Global Affair" proposes that the nations of the world should think of the world's children when dealing with the immense international problems of our time.

4.   Can a Leopard Change Its Spots?

Another way of expressing the need for learning what is right and unlearning of what is wrong is to say that there is a need for character improvement. The real questions are, then, "Can character be trained?" "Can a man change his ways which have become his very self?" In other words, "Can a leopard change its spots?" Let us consider this matter as presented in a motion picture featuring Burt Lancaster.

"The Leopard"

Text: And the wolf shall dwell with the lamb;
        and the leopard shall lie down with the kid . . .

—Isaiah 11:6

For the earth shall be full of the knowledge of the
Lord, as the waters cover the sea

—ibid. 11:9

Can the Ethiopian change his skin, or the leopard
his spots?
Then may ye also do good that are accustomed to do
evil.

—Jeremiah 13:23

A serious difference of opinion seems to exist between Isaiah
and Jeremiah, two of the most important prophets in the history
of mankind. Using poetic imagery, Isaiah preaches that as it is
possible for a leopard to lose its instinct to kill its prey, so it is
conceivable that man will lose his depravity and dwell in peace
with his neighbors.

Jeremiah seems to think otherwise, saying that as a leopard
cannot change its spots, so man cannot change his animal nature causing him to act evilly.

The difference between the two great prophets is more apparent than real. Isaiah would agree with Jeremiah that the
task is most difficult. Jeremiah on the other hand would agree
with his older colleague that in the ultimate future man will
conquer his animal nature. For that great day to come, much
education is needed along with God's loving intervention.

An interesting motion picture, "The Leopard", a recent international prize winner, presents what is the un-Biblical view
of things in this regard. The foreword to the film declares:
"Things will have to change in order to remain the same." Burt
Lancaster, as the Italian Prince, observing the social changes in
the Italy of Garibaldi, maintains that regardless what revolu-
tions take place, society will always have its leopards and jackals.
Those who enact these roles may differ, but the roles remain
the same.

Against this theory is the faith of the prophets which maintains that man can, and will tame the leopard that lurks within.

C. PROPER PERSPECTIVES

1. Reading In and Reading Out

In moral education, we come face to face with vital and involved problems. How to discover what is right—to see it steadily

and whole in a society that is constantly changing—is no simple matter.

Take the matter of utilizing the Bible as a standard book for ethical instruction. Even granted that it is practical to utilize the Bible for ethical instruction, how can we be sure that the instructor knows how to interpret it properly? A group of young Englishmen in a topical revue alerted us to the danger of a wrong interpretation leading to wrong conduct.

"The Cambridge Circus"

Text: Joshua said unto the people: "Shout, for the
        Lord hath given you the city".

—Joshua 6:16

"The Cambridge Circus", an English musical review, derives its name from the opening scene. The company of seven males and one female, appear as participants in a circus show.

The young lady, dressed as an animal trainer, equipped even with a whip, puts the young men of the troupe through paces as if they were performing animals. At the snap of her whip some behave as trained dogs, others as dancing horses, and one even as an elephant. When the latter ponderously lifts one foot and holds it precariously over the young lady's head, just as the trick might be done in a real-life circus, the humor of the situation shines forth.

Although the review is essentially slapstick spoofing, it is in place to consider the point of this comic situation. We realize that when animals are trained to show signs of intelligence, we are impressed. When we see human beings acting like animals who reveal the rudiments of human intelligence, then we laugh. It is this twist that makes the action ludicrous, and therefore funny.

A similar comic situation in the review is presented when a performer enacts someone who might have been a radio announcer in Biblical times reporting Biblical events. The fall of Jericho, he reports in his best radio announcer's voice, is "rumored to have been caused by the air waves caused by the horns blaring around the walls of the city". David, he says in another newscast, weighed in at so many stones (an English term for a weight of fourteen pounds) and Goliath at one stone less. "This stone", he says, "may prove crucial in the encounter".

Although "The Cambridge Circus" only meant to produce a laugh with this—and indeed does succeed—the fact is that it issues a warning to those who would make Biblical events and ideas relevant to our times not to overlook the real historic differences in thought and modes of action between the past and the present.

Failure to keep this in mind can make a circus even out of the Bible.

2. Faithless Translations

Having a wrong slant on life can even lead to seeing in the Bible a way of life which denies the very spirit of Scriptures! Selfishness breeds a self-centeredness and disregard for others' rights which frequently are at the heart of human wickedness. An example of this can be found in one of Shirley MacLaine's pictures.

"What a Way to Go"

Text: And Thou shalt love thy neighbor as thyself.
                                           —Leviticus 19:18

There are at least two Biblical references in the movie, "What a Way To Go". One of them is to the effect that seeking financial success too assiduously can cause the loss of many valuable things, including life itself. This idea is suggested by the title. It is, however, so obvious that it requires hardly any comment.

There is a second Biblical allusion, on the other hand, which deserves our attention. In one of the scenes, Shirley MacLaine's screen mother is shown to be a type of person who has an interesting kind of religiosity.

On this lady's living room wall is hung the Biblical axiom: "Thou shalt love thy neighbor as thyself." Through a camera effect, the way in which she reads and interprets this high ethical and religious principle is shown.

The words, "thou shalt . . . thy neighbor as" are dropped, so that all that is left of the maxim is: "Love . . . thyself". Here the point is made dramatically that reading and quoting the Bible is not enough. What is important is how the Bible is interpreted.

Often in life we find people who translate the Bible in such a way as to distort its meaning. This mistranslation when it is from one language to another is bad enough. It becomes rotten when the Bible, though quoted, is misread and misapplied from language into real life to the hurt of people.

Since to love one's neighbor as oneself has come to be accepted as the cardinal principle of the ethical life, to distort its Biblical meaning so as just to love oneself is a major sin. Shakespeare has an allusion to its gravity in Sonnet 62:

> Sin of self-love possesseth all mine eye,
> And all my soul, and all my every part.

Credit must be given to "What a Way To Go" for showing graphically the way the religious principle of love of neighbor as oneself can be abused.

3a. Love Thyself

Since a man must take care of himself, be independent, morally responsible, etc. over-emphasis on his personal interests are an ever-present possibility. Sometimes the results are not as serious as humorous. A case like this has been the subject of a Jean Kerr play.

"King of Hearts"

Text: Only take heed to thyself, and keep thy
       soul diligently . . .
                                        —Deuteronomy 4:9

What is the proper way to regard and to deal with man's natural concern for his own welfare?

A certain amount of selfishness is necessary for every human being. If a man does not take care of himself, who will? The failure of a man to be independent and self-supporting can be disastrous.

On the other hand, too great an emphasis on one's own selfish interests can lead to a disintegration not only of all social living but of the individual personality itself. The Bible stressed the need for a proper balance between "selfishness" and "selflessness" for wholesome living. A later classic formulation of this polarity of the human personality put it in this way: "If I am not for me, who will be? If I am only for myself, what am I?"

A humorous treatment of an aspect of this theme has been provided by the very gifted playwright, Jean Kerr, in her "King of Hearts". Featuring Henry Morgan, a fine cast presented this play at the Bergen Mall Playhouse the other week.

The story is of a cartoonist who in spite of his professed interest in promoting the happiness and welfare of human beings —especially children—is concerned really only with himself. Egoistic to the point of being egotistic, the cartoonist makes a ludicrous picture.

Actually, he is not an evil person. He is not vicious in his selfishness, as so many people unfortunately are. Completely devoted to himself, convinced of his unique gifts, he cavalierly disregards the sentiments of others associated with him. In his opinion, which he regards as infallible, he is the greatest artist and human being. The title of the play—"King of Hearts" —suggests what he really is. He is just a card.

3. b. Love Thyself

Nearly always where there is abuse of one's fellow human beings, the perpetrator of the cruelty may be assumed to be indulging in improper self-love. Indeed, it might very well be self-hate. The famous novel—now a film—"Billy Budd" has pointed this out.

"Billy Budd"

Text: And thou shalt love thy neighbor as thyself . . .
—Leviticus 19:18

The love of neighbor has come to be accepted as one of the two basic requirements of the Judeo-Christian way of life. The other is the love of God.

Since this principle of love of neighbor is so basic and universally recognized as right, a good question is: Why has it not been practiced more?

Some would say that it is opposed to human nature and therefore difficult to observe. Others maintain that on the contrary it is completely in keeping with man's spirit, except that it is not given a chance because of conditions. Some argue that love of neighbor is not practiced because people do not understand its meaning.

In connection with this last idea, the moving picture "Billy Budd" based on the famous novel of the same name—that of its hero—has something of interest to tell its viewers. In one of the scenes pictured aboard ship, the sailor Billy Budd, expressed his opinion of and to the master-at-arms, who is a cruel and vindictive individual. "The trouble with you," says Billy, "is that you hate yourself. Therefore, you can not love others". The point made here is that in order to love one's neighbor as one's self, one must first love one's self properly.

It does happen frequently that a person frustrated in his own life, and disgusted with himself, comes to hate his fellowmen upon whom he seeks to divest himself of his frustrations.

He who is at peace with himself is more likely to be at peace with his neighbors.

When Billy Budd is hanged at the end of the picture, he is to be seen as a victim not only of those who hated him, but also as a victim of those who hated themselves.

4. Morality's Shifting Perspectives

One of the phrases in the human vocabulary that reflects a basic truth about human values is the one that consists of two words: "It depends". So often what is wrong in one case, is proper in another, and vice-versa. "It depends" on circumstances and the people involved whether an action or word is right or wrong. A memorable presentation of an aspect of this truth has been given on Broadway by an English troupe.

"Chips with Everything"

Text: So I prophesied as He commanded me and the breath

came into them, and they lived, and stood up upon
their feet, an exceeding great Army.

—Ezekiel 37:10

In his mind's eye, the prophet Ezekiel envisions a valley full
of dry bones, utterly lifeless. By the power of God's intervention, these bones become covered with flesh and skin, are restored to life, and form the components of a tremendous army.
The point is made by this prophecy, that through God's Will
the people who had appeared completely destroyed could be
restored to Glory. An interesting and surprising thing to note
is that the condition of this reconstituted Nation is given as
that of an Army.

Does not an "army" imply along with thoughts of power and
victory, also the concept of warfare? Is not war the very denial
of the future ideal situation which is described by the prophet
himself as a "covenant of peace" between God and the People?

Obviously, as with all analogies, the comparison of the People
to an Army is meant to be taken with certain reservations.

Even more obviously, the virtues and the "reservations" of
the moral code of the peacetime British Air Force are the subject of a current Broadway play imported from England, "Chips
With Everything".

The training of R.A.F. recruits reveals the good and bad sides
of the "traditions of the service". For example, one leader says,
"We will teach you discipline and obedience". That is all right.
Not so right is the instruction of another officer who barks
"Don't speak when you answer me!"

Chips (potatoes) with everything, the food fare of the young
soldiers, does not make for the most appetizing meals. Even
more unpalatable and undigestible is swallowing whole the
idea that the military version of morality (perhaps necessary
in war-time) is without a blemish in time of peace.

IV

The Elusive, Fascinating Nature
of Man

Man—Animal But Social

If there were a "Hit Parade" for questions, the question, "What is Man?" would rank among the all-time favorites. It is understandable that universally and for the longest time, this question has been raised—and it is being asked just as widely and frequently today as ever—for the answer to it concerns the life and well-being of every human being and society as a whole.

The fact is that the answer to the question has been and is being given in many, many ways. The reason for this is that man's nature is as fascinating as it is difficult to grasp. Much before and ever since Socrates said "Know thyself", every man has been trying to understand himself; yet, self-knowledge continues to be an illusive thing.

Even though Aristotle expressed a deep and abiding truth about the fundamental nature of man, the full meaning of man's character still eludes us. The great Greek philosophers' description of man as being a "social animal" only indicates how involved, contradictory, and complex, are those characteristics called human.

The picture of these qualities of what man is and ought to be is called "man's image". Aspects of this image of man as presented in contemporary plays, and as seen from the point of view of the Bible, will be described in this chapter. For example, the reader will find here the Arthur Miller concept that man is essentially a sinner, along with other statements by other playwrights in which human nature is differently conceived. All in all, these concepts of the nature of man, and of his values and ideals, are significant, because they are reflected ultimately in the conduct and attitudes of human beings in real life situations.

A. A LITTLE LOWER THAN THE ANGELS

1. What Is Man?

a. A Sinner

What a man is, so he thinks; what a man thinks, so he is. Moreover, what a man conceives to be the nature of his fellow human beings plays a great part in determining how he treats them. If a man thinks of his neighbors as tools, he uses them; if as men made in God's image, and therefore of inestimable worth, he deals with them differently. The truth is that a study of the behavior of mankind reveals what Aristotle suggested, namely that man has both a bestial and spiritual nature. That the higher and nobler element in man's make-up can and should become the guide and way of life for mankind is expressed in the Biblical idea that man has been endowed by his Creator with this potentiality, for he was made "a little lower than the angels". How this possibility and the values inherent in it have been expressed in the world, has been an on-going theme for many a modern playwright, including of course, Arthur Miller. Mr. Miller's answer to the question: "What is Man?" as given in one of his recent plays, is based on an interpretation of the Holy Scriptures.

"After the Fall"

Text: And He said: "Who told thee that thou wast naked? Hast thou eaten of the tree, whereof I commanded thee that thou shouldst not eat?"
—Genesis 3:11

It is a wise playwright who knows his own play. Arthur Miller, accordingly, is not only a skillful, but an unusually wise author.

Just how understanding and honest he is in expressing his meaning have been severely questioned by a host of critics dealing with his play, "After the Fall". Although Mr. Miller has allowed that every writer must necessarily write from his own experiences, he has strictly denied that his play is autobiographical.

No, says Mr. Miller, the Maggie of his play is not the Marilyn Monroe he knew, married and divorced in real life! "How can he say that?" question the critics who see an unmistakable resemblance between the ill-starred Maggie and the equally unfortunate, once-starred Marilyn.

Whatever the situation is in this matter, there can be no mistaking what Mr. Miller means to convey in and through his play in a larger sense. It is clearly set forth by the author in his own foreword to "After the Fall".

The striking thing about this statement of the meaning of his work is the clear-cut Biblical references that Mr. Miller makes in it. Mr. Miller writes in part: "The first real 'story' in the Bible is the murder of Abel. Before this drama there is only a featureless Paradise. But in that Eden there was peace because man had no consciousness of himself nor any knowledge of sex or his separateness from plants or other animals. Presumably we are being told that the human being becomes 'himself' in the act of becoming aware of his sinfulness. He 'is' what he is ashamed of."

This short citation from his foreword is enough to indicate how Mr. Miller regards his play as having a Biblical tone. What else should we expect when the very title, "After the Fall", is derived from the Bible?

b.   A Good Personality

The idea that Man is essentially a sinner who has fallen from Grace, is of course, a theological one. Whether this is the true nature of Man has been the subject of much debate, arising out of deep differences of opinion and resulting in the organization of various theological systems of thought. In our modern world, where theology does not seem to be emphasized as much as previously, since the sciences—physical and social—have come to the fore, another view of Man has become popular. It is that he is a personality. Just what is meant by personality, and how it functions, has itself become a matter of investigation, especially in the fields of psychology, sociology and ethics. An entertaining musical comedy starring Robert Preston has had some interesting insights to offer in this regard.

"The Music Man"

Text: And the Lord God called unto the man,
       and said unto him: "Where art thou"?

—Genesis 3:9

The famous divine question directed to Adam, calling him to face up to his failure to heed God's prohibition of the eating from the fruit of the Tree of Knowledge implies that more is to be expected of man than from any of God's other creations.

In other words, the human differential which is man's "personality" gives man his dignity and special place in the scheme of things.

The word, "personality", has come only comparatively recently into common usage. Interestingly, along with its fundamental meaning there has been added another implication which is widely used. This second interpretation renders the word "personality" as referring to a quality of behavior which makes a man or woman well liked. Thus, we say: "So and so has personality", meaning that he is charming and popular.

The question which often presents itself in our every day experience is: does "personality" in the original sense of human nature calling for good and righteous conduct have any reference to its second meaning of popularity and acceptance by the group?

In Meredith Wilson's "The Music Man" we come face to face with one aspect of this involved question. "Professor" Harold Hill, the music man, is possessed of a winning personality but his lack of honesty detracts from his human personality. In this beloved play everything works out well in the end when along with admitting the error of his ways, Harold Hill is shown to be a fundamentally decent human being.

This then is the sum of the matter. A person is best loved not only because of the music of a capitivating personality, but also, and more so, because of the qualities of an inspiring character. An aggregation of "seventy-six trombones" might well proclaim this basic truth of the Music Man.

2. Who Shall Rule Over Man?

"Is man a human personality owing allegiance primarily to other human beings, or does he trail clouds of glory in the sense of having divine attributes and obligations mainly"? is a vital question, the answers to which have led to various ramifications. Many centuries ago, this question and its answer had something to do with determining the form of political organization in ancient Israel, for one thing. Similarly, the framework of modern states has been determined in part by how the question "What is Man?" was answered. A play, and also a movie, about a celebrated English Archbishop highlight this situation which has most modern implications.

"Becket"

Text: And the Lord said unto Samuel: "Hearken unto the voice of the people in all that they say to thee; for they have not rejected thee, but they have rejected Me, that I should not be King over them". . . And the Lord said to Samuel: "Hearken unto their voice and make them a king."

—I Samuel 8:7, 22

In our day the relationship between Church and State is an issue which has quite a few serious subissues. In the United States, various questions concerning religion and the schools are raised. May religion be taught in the public schools? May prayers be recited in such schools? Have parochial schools a just claim for State support?

Outside the United States there are objections being offered to the idea of an official State religion with the consequent relegating to inferior if not illegal positions of other religions. Communism, of course, regards religion as an opiate of the people and suppresses it.

All over the question is: does religion have the right to "mix" in politics?

These questions and others may implicitly be brought to mind upon considering "Becket"—the play by Anouilh recently made into a movie. Thomas Becket, as Archbishop of England, opposed the right of King Henry II to deprive ecclesiastical courts of certain of their functions. Ultimately, Becket is murdered and the King establishes the power of the State over the Church. Much before the days of King Henry—even in Biblical times —the question of the power of the human king (the State) vis-a-vis the Divine King (the Church) was of burning moment. When Samuel, the prophet, anointed Saul as King over Israel, he foresaw the troublesome situation which was to ensue in his time and for generations to come. Thomas Becket was one of the victims—or shall we say martyrs?—of that disturbing question: "Who shall rule over men?"

3. Who Shall Fully Judge Man?

Whether man is considered mainly in terms of psychology as "a personality" or whether he is conceived chiefly in the idiom of religion as a "child of God", the simple truth is that it requires superhuman ability to understand his nature completely. We may see this humbling truth suggested in a Cary Grant vehicle.

"Charade"

Text: Man looks into the eyes,
       but God looks into the heart.

—I Samuel 16:7

Can it be that the one or ones who gave the title to the movie made an error? The film to which I am referring is called "Charade".

Now, everyone knows that "charade" is the name of a game where the object is to guess what or who is meant by figuring out the silent gesturing of one's partner. In other words, the effort is not to disguise but to reveal without actually saying so.

A current motion picture, starring Cary Grant and Katherine Hepburn, is entitled "Charade". As this movie develops everything is done in it to confuse and confound both the cast of players and the audience so that the mystery and suspense are maintained and heightened.

In the telling of its story, "Charade" deals with puzzling murders in such a way as to make them appear more baffling. Furthermore, to confound confusion, corpses are made the subjects of humor.

One thing is certain about "Charade". Nothing in it is to be taken seriously. Even its title is suspect. As is said about the hero, so may it be posited about the movie, "Serious, that is the last word he wants to hear".

For all of this, there is an interesting idea which may come to mind almost as an idea arrived at through a game of charades. The picture suggests without saying so that much of human life is a guessing game about the nature of people's characters.

Words and actions are used to reflect a person's personality. Can we be sure, however, about these as legitimate indices of character? Is there not always the matter of the inner spirit which is so difficult to grasp?

As was said clearly centuries ago, so does the strangely titled moving picture "Charade" say indirectly today: "Man looks into the eyes, but God looks into the heart."

4. Depravity of Human Nature

a. Drunkardness

Even though man cannot fully understand himself or his neighbors—this knowledge surpasses human understanding—it must be clear to everyone that there is in human nature "a lower and a higher self". It is saddening to observe how people frequently forfeit their higher to their lower impulses. Not in harsh criticism, but with regret, we may see all about us those who have fallen victim to drunkardness, for example. A play with a strange title recently told a story of this only too familiar truth.

"Never Live Over a Pretzel Factory"

Text: Happy art thou, O land, when thy king is a free man,
And thy princes eat in due season,
In strength, and not in drunkenness.
—Ecclesiastes 10:17

"Never Live Over a Pretzel Factory" is the title of a play that recently had its world premiere at the Playhouse on the Mall.

Part of the fun is to understand the reason for this title. Suffice it to say that the phrase is a bit of advice. Seeing the play in the light of the Bible (which may not have been the author's intent at all) offers much more serious counsel than hits the eye.

The story concerns a movie star who has the bad habit of going on a drunken binge whenever he is about to start shooting a picture. In such a condition, he happens upon three young men who live in a basement of a building that is marked for destruction because of urban renewal.

Learning of their plan to produce a small documentary concerning loneliness in the big city of New York, he flamboyantly suggests that they should think big. Instead of producing this film to cost five-thousand dollars, he offers to help them finance and produce it at a much larger cost. Before his proposition can materialize—it never does—his drunkenness leads to episodes and involvements which may appear hilarious on the stage.

In real life, however, there is tragedy abundant in a situation where a modern cinema king or queen has come to be associated with an existence that is marked by drunkenness and infidelity. The tragedy is not only for the star, but for society.

"Never Live Over a Pretzel Factory" probably was intended by its author just to be a riotous comedy. Since comedy and tragedy are so closely related, however, it is in place to consider that the title implies further that twisted lives can never be really happy.

b.   The Sweet Life

A syndrome of sin may be said to be the subject matter of a motion picture, "La Dolce Vita", which has become famous. So well-known, indeed, is the film that its title has become a phrase by which society as a whole—not only that of modern Rome which is the locale of the film—is being described and identified. In this description of "The Sweet Life" can be seen how much lower than the angels man can descend.

"La Dolce Vita"

Text: There shall not be found among you one that maketh his son or daughter to pass through the fire,

> one that useth divination, a soothsayer or an
> enchanter, or a sorcerer, or a charmer, or one that
> consulteth a ghost or a familiar spirit, or a
> necromancer.
>
> —Deuteronomy 18:11

The Bible objected forcefully to any and all forms of superstition. Yet for all its antagonism there have been kept in the Biblical tradition references to the so-called "evil eye".

As with every piece of superstition, so also with this one concerning the evil eye, there is an element of truth in it.

It is dangerous, for example, to walk under a ladder, whether bad luck follows or not. The "evil eye" in its meaning of greed and lust is rife with danger for human beings.

The recent moving picture "La Dolce Vita", which has come to be a symbol of moral decadence, has an interesting reference to the "evil eye". In one of its last scenes, a group of revellers find a strange-looking fish which has been washed up on the beach. What is most striking about it is the kind of eyes it has. They seem to be staring at everyone, and yet at no one. Each eye has a malevolent quality about it. This "evil eye" is meant to symbolize what has gone wrong with society.

Interested in greedy and lustful satisfactions, moral virtues have been discarded by the debauchers. Seen with an "evil eye" the world is meant for vice.

"La Dolce Vita" has given its name to a type of society. The evil eye is that society's coat of arms. It is interesting that in the film so many of the characters wear dark glasses day and night, indoors and outdoors. Their eyes are sensitive to the light. They are evil.

c. The Sweet Child

The tendency to evil is something that man has within him from birth. A fine play has been written on the theme of perversity which appears even in children.

"The Innocents"

Text: The inclination of man's heart is evil
       from his youth . . .

—Genesis 8:21

Joshua Loth Liebman in his famous book, "Peace of Mind", published some years back, expressed the idea that little children are not as innocent as they look. Actually, Liebman explained, there are even in the infant urges and impulses which are selfish, and one might almost say nasty.

This idea has been expressed centuries before in the Bible. "The inclination of man's heart is evil from his youth."

In a splendid play, "The Innocents" by William Archibald based on "The Turn of the Screw" by Henry James, this theme is treated as a kind of mystery or ghost story. Superbly acted by Betsy Palmer and Elena Karam, in association with two exceptionally gifted child stars, Sindee Ann Richards and John Megna, it was recently presented at the Playhouse on the Mall.

The story tells of a governess charged with the upbringing of two children who, she becomes convinced, are not such "innocents". The little boy is completely possessed with the desire to do evil. The little girl is bad but corrigible.

The housekeeper just hopes everything will be all right. The governess, however, sets herself actively to freeing the boy from his wickedness. She succeeds, but at what a cost! She says to the boy: "Miles, now you have goodness and kindness. You are free!" At that moment she discovers that the child has died.

Does this mean simply that training for adulthood must bring the destruction of the youthful life of folly and foible? Does it mean that there can be no human life without an evil inclination? Where then does this evil come from? Is it inherited, or does it come from evil spirits about us?

As with every ghost story, great room is left to each individual's imagination.

5. Evil Is Real

In the complicated questions, "What is Life?" and "What is Man?" the concepts of good and evil are very much involved. Sometimes it has been maintained by philosophers that since God created the world, and He is all-good, that which is evil only appears so; it has no real existence. Sometimes it has been argued that since evil is a relative term, and what may be wrong for one person may be right for another, it has no reality. For all of this, it should ever be kept in mind that evil is a real thing, and must be dealt with as such.

"Can Can"

Text: And the eyes of them both were opened,
and they knew that they were naked,
and they sewed fig leaves together,
and made themselves girdles.

—Genesis 3:7

The Scriptures tell us that Adam and Eve experienced no shame in being naked until Satan came along and "put them wise". In other words, it was the evil mind of Satan which planted thoughts of immodesty in the conscience of man and woman. Were it not for satanic ideas, there would be nothing shameful about an undressed human body.

The French have the words for this, saying: "Mal y soit qui mal y pense." He who thinks evil of something innocent betrays himself as being evil.

This French idiom has been accepted as a by-word even among English speaking peoples. It is not strange then, that a famous musical comedy dealing with this theme has its locale in the Montmartre section of Paris.

The play, "Can Can" tells of a Madame Pistache, who with her dancing girls teaches a judge among others that there is nothing shameful in having a "good time".

A high point in this musical is a scene danced in pantomime featuring Eve, Satan and the famous Apple. It is precisely this scene, however, which causes the beholder to wonder whether a thing is evil only because someone regards it as such.

Since the gates of Paradise were shut, society has developed standards for its morality. Although the music is beautiful—Cole Porter was never better—the play's point remains suspect. How else could it be what with Madame Pistache and her girls serving as Principal and Faculty in a School for Morals?

"Mal y soit" applies only to something innocent. Madame Pistache would laugh out loud at such a preposterous claim for herself. Really, a "good time" is not necessarily good.

6. Human Nature as a Symphony

Human nature, as Life itself, is complex. Good and evil, the
call of the Spirit and the call of the wild, man's higher and
lower self, are in constant opposition, flux and tension. What
may help one to unravel the complexity is to consider life and
human nature as a symphony, with a point of virtue, a counterpoint of villainy, and a final resolution for good. See how the
musical based on Charles Dickens' great book reflects this idea.

"Oliver"

Text: Holy, holy, holy is the Lord of Hosts;
        The whole earth is full of His glory.

—Isaiah 6:5

        Then said I:
        "Woe is me for I am undone;
        Because I am a man of unclean lips,
        And I dwell in the midst of a people of unclean
        lips . . ."

—ibid. 6:5

One Englishman, Charles Dickens, wrote a novel calling it
"Oliver Twist". Another Englishman, Lionel Bart, a century
later, wrote the book, music and lyrics of a play based on that
novel calling it just plain "Oliver".

This "Oliver" after first being produced in England is currently on Broadway as "a musical".

It is not exactly a musical comedy. We cannot describe it as
an operetta, and certainly not as an opera. It can perhaps be
considered as a play with music.

The music is especially tuneful and beautiful. Although the
music is not at all that of a symphony, it does suggest that the
play itself may be understood best in the musical idiom of a
symphony. As with the symphonic form, the play "Oliver" has
a point, a counterpoint, and a resolution of both.

The point or theme of the play is literally blazened forth in
the opening scene where a banner bears the words, "God is
Love". The counterpoint to this theme of love—human and
divine—is man's inhumanity to his fellow man. What happens
to Oliver Twist and those about him is the carrying out of this
point and counterpoint with their final resolution.

Isaiah, the greatest of prophets in the eighth century B.C.E. recognized this symphonic-like quality of life with its major theme of God's Holiness offset by the counterpoint of man's sinfulness.

Ours must be the faith of an Isaiah in response to an Oliver's plaintive query, "Where is Love?" that ultimately it will be revealed fully and abundantly as the waters cover the sea.

B. FRIENDLINESS

1. Gratitude—a Many Splendored Thing

"Give me friendship, or give me death", said an ancient Hebrew sage. In this statement there is the unmistakable recognition by all of us of the truth that human life without sociability or friendliness has lost a good deal of its worth.

In accepting this concept of friendship as a basic value, we should consider how it is derived, and how it expresses itself best. Tradition has much to tell us about these, even as the modern theatre has concerned itself a great deal in this area.

Considering how our lives are enriched and made meaningful by the friendships we enjoy, and by the social contacts through which we have our being (no human life is possible without society) we have reason to be grateful for these. To be ungrateful is to be unfriendly. It is, in a sense, to die spiritually. There is such a message in a popular musical comedy.

"The Unsinkable Molly Brown"

Text: Take . . . my gift because God hath dealt
        graciously with me.
                                            —Genesis 53:11

Gratitude is an important human quality with a number of phases. There is, for example, gratitude to God as well as gratitude to one's fellowmen. There is the matter of being gracious in accepting favors. There is the truth that at times people are ungrateful for what they have because they are jealous of what others have. These are but few of the phases of gratitude which one might do well to consider. The Bible in one instance gives a beautiful illustration of how Jacob expressed his thankfulness to God for the many blessings he enjoyed by offering to share them with his estranged brother Esau.

An enjoyable contemporary musical comedy, "The Unsinkable Molly Brown", presented recently at the Papermill Playhouse, might also be considered as providing a lesson of the spirit in the matter of being grateful. The heroine, Molly Brown, from poor, hardy, untutored folk has become rich because of her husband's gold strike. Finding herself in the company of other wealthy folk she teaches them the propriety of sharing their wealth—God-given—with the Church and the poor. Since God has been open-handed with them, she declares, these rich should be generous to Him and His causes.

As a musical comedy, it may not be expected that full character developments of the players be provided. The audience can not know, therefore, whether the attitude of generous thanksgiving implanted in this cultured social has been set firmly and completely.

What is revealed, though, is that even Molly Brown, while indeed grateful to God, has been ungrateful at the same time to her own folk. Finally, however, Molly is shown to have achieved a higher cultivation than mere social manners. She has cultivated the quality of gratitude not only to God but to her spouse and her people as well. Having become less unsinkable, she has grown far more lovable.

2.   Between People of Different Races

a.   History is Made

In present-day America the matter of friendship, of sociability, of gratitude, is not something for discussion in a parlor or sitting-room only. Today, these things are burning issues around which extremists rally and by which the majority of Americans are torn and seriously affected, for these are of the essence of the Negroes' claims for full equality and total freedom in the United States and all over the world.

The theatre, not surprisingly, has been both stage on which and arena in which the drama of civil rights has been fought and enacted. A first in the history of the American Theatre and in the civil rights movement has come into existence only recently.

"The Owl and the Pussy Cat"

Text: Are ye not as the children of the Ethiopians unto Me,
O children of Israel? saith the Lord . . .

—Amos 9:7

"The Owl and the Pussy Cat" with a two character cast may well live in history. If it achieves this memorable status, it will not be because of its story, its writing, its situations—all of which are fun-producing but not fame-evoking. It will come about because for the first time in the modern "legitimate" theatre, casting was made without regard to a prejudice about the color of an actor's skin.

The story concerns two young people—a man and a woman—who are thrown together, and then find that love unites them. The girl who has been plying the oldest profession in the world is forced to move from her apartment by her landlord. This worthy was alerted to her activity by a neighbor, a young man who was spying on her (his name is Felix). It is into the latter's apartment that the girl, Doris, forces her way. Once there, she makes herself at home. In a short time, Felix, the Owl (with a name like that you would imagine he was the Cat) and Doris, the Pussy Cat are in love.

The situation, the dialogue and the acting are all fine and laugh-provoking. What makes the play memorable, however, is the fact that this girl's role happens to be played by a Negress, Diane Sand. That this part could have been enacted by a white actress—indeed, Miss Sand's standby is white—makes for the historic situation. For the first time in the contemporary theatre—where the actor's skin coloration was immaterial for the development of the play, no thought was given to the matter!

"The Owl and the Pussy Cat"—this modest two character comedy—is fulfilling a Biblical teaching in a new and important way.

It does proclaim, in practice, Amos' proposition that all people are equal in God's sight. For this, it deserves a special place in the annals of the theatre and in the history of Humanity.

b. White vs. Black and Vice-Versa

It is to be expected that the contemporary American Theatre should reflect the burning issue of the day—the struggle for equality and complete freedom for and by the Negroes. Jean Genet, a French writer, has described in moving terms this troublesome condition (1'). Ossie Davis, an American playwright and actor, emphasized in comic, but telling phrases and situations the essential justice of the American Negroes' cause which has a Biblical basis (2'). Langston Hughes, an American poet, calls attention similarly to the righteousness of the demand for freedom which is Biblically endorsed (3'). From South Africa has come a play which suggests how difficult and wrought with danger the issue is (4'). James Baldwin, novelist turned playwright, in his first Broadway play, sees the solution to the problem as coming through Negro violence, if need be (5').

1'.

"The Blacks"

Text: Are ye not like the Ethiopians unto me,
        O people of Israel? saith the Lord.
        Did I not bring up Israel from the land of Egypt,
        and the Philistines from Caphtor,
        and the Syrians from Kir?

                                                —Amos 9:7

Every book, every chapter, verse and letter contained in the Holy Bible partakes of the quality of sanctity. Some of these, however, have become more sanctified than others in the human consciousness. There are a number of verses, for example, which have become the basic texts of mankind's striving to be human. Thus we may designate as "key texts" such lines as these: "Love thy neighbor as thyself". "What doth the Lord require of thee? But to do justly, to love mercy, and to walk humbly with thy God."

Another verse that has been singled out for special sanctity is one that is especially timely in these days of revolution for civil rights. It is the line from Amos declaring that in regard to freedom, no people is more God-chosen than any other. God is the Power that makes for Freedom and as such, throughout history, God has made Himself manifest as the Father of all His children, yearning to breathe free.

How simple and clear are the ideas and directives for human action in this verse of Amos. On the other hand, how involved and complicated are the beliefs and practices of mankind in matters of equality, freedom and justice for all races!

A current off-Broadway play by the French writer, Jean Genet, is remarkable for its success in capturing and conveying this terribly muddled condition in which Negroes and whites find themselves all over the world. Called "The Blacks" the play does not follow a simple logical development of plot. Being a reflection of the real-life situation, it purposely does not.

Genet's play, filled with symbolism, shockingly portrays how unfortunately distant from Amos is the thought today of many a White on Black, and Black on White.

2'.

"Purlie Victorious"

Text: Then Shadrach, Meshach, and Abed-nego came forth
        out of the midst of the fire.
                                                   —Daniel 3:26

Next to the story of the exodus from Egypt, Negro spirituals seem to have made the account of Daniel and his companions in the fiery furnace a central theme. In both cases there is enslavement—something which the Negro knew at first hand. In both cases there is ultimate freedom—something for which the Negro heart yearns. Both in the escape from the waters of the Red Sea and the deliverance from the fires of Babylon there is firm faith in the God of Israel as Saviour. The Negro folksongs have earned their name as spirituals, precisely because of this self-same faith they proclaim.

A recent Broadway play, "Purlie Victorious", now appearing as a movie, "Gone Are The Days", written by Ossie Davis, has all the qualities of a spiritual, plus the earthiness of a true-to-life portrayal. The play abounds with humorous, and yet not so funny truths. "Being colored can be lots of fun when nobody is looking." "I have race pride but I don't need it much in my

line of work." "I find in being black a secret cup of gladness."
The interesting thing about the play is that like a Negro
spiritual, it is essentially Biblical. The church which the hero,
Purlie Victorious, aims to redeem as a sign of Negro emanci-
pation is Beth El. This name in Biblical Hebrew means House
of God.

That this play should have such strong Biblical overtones is
not surprising when one considers how completely the history
of ancient Israel has been made the history of the Negro. When
the Negro sings of Egypt or of Babylon it is as if he had been
there.

To see Ossie Davis and his charming wife, Ruby Dee and
the rest of their company in "Purlie Victorious" is in a real
sense to see part of the Bible on Broadway.

3'.

"Jericho Jim Crow"

Text: . . . And it came to pass that when the people
        heard the sound of the horn,
        that the people shouted with a great shout,
        and the wall fell down flat . . .
                                            —Joshua 6:20

Strictly speaking, it is not a play. It is not presented on Broadway, or even on what is commonly known as off-Broadway. The
auditorium where it is played is not a theatre, but a Sanctuary.
The Sanctuary is not that of a church alone, or a synagogue
alone, but of both.

For all of that, it may well be reckoned a most dramatic
offering worthy of Broadway. Its name is "Jericho Jim Crow",
written by Langston Hughes, and it is being presented in the
Sanctuary of the Brotherhood Synagogue and of the Village
Presbyterian Church which share a Sanctuary together at 143
West 13th Street in New York City.

In this production, Jim Crowism is associated with the walls
of Jericho, mentioned in the Bible. In Holy Writ, we are told
that the walls of this Canaanite city came tumbling down after
the Hebrew people had encircled it, singing, shouting and
sounding horns for seven days.

In "Jericho Jim Crow" one witnesses a group of gifted actors and singers who describe in action and in dialogue and song the American Negroes' struggle for freedom and equality. The actors have very little scenery to help them in their efforts.

This may be taken to be a very part of its moving message. There has been little indeed on the American scene to encourage the Negroes in their struggle. Their own voices have been the decisive factor in toppling the walls of segregation and inequality.

Their own voices have been effective, it is true. It is also true that the faith and the ideals which gave given power and meaning to their words have stemmed from the Bible. One of the leading characters puts it succinctly when he exclaims: "If you believe that I am Joshua, then I am!"

4'.

"The Blood Knot"

Text: And the Lord said unto Cain: "Where is Abel,
thy brother?" And he said: "I know not;
am I my brother's keeper?"
And He said: "What hast thou done? The voice of thy
brother's blood crieth unto Me from the ground."
—Genesis 4:9, 10

"The Blood Knot" is a brilliant play being presented just as brilliantly at the off-Broadway Cricket Theater. Its story is disarmingly simple.

In Port Elizabeth, South Africa today, two half-brothers born of the same Negro mother, but one with a Negro father and the other with a white father, are sharing together a ramshackle hut. Morris Pieterson, whose father was white, has a light skin, while Zachariah, his half-brother is black. The latter works hard to earn the little money which his half-brother is saving for them so that some day in the future they can buy a farm.

This plan for their future is difficult to consummate because Zachariah, with a zeal for living in the present, especially yearns for female companionship.

To check him in this longing, his white brother influences him to turn to a female pen-pal instead of one in the flesh. The matter becomes involved when it develops that the pen-pal is a white girl who intends to visit Zachariah, a Negro. That this should happen in South Africa is unthinkable and fraught with danger.

When Morris tries to explain this to his black brother, the searing conflict in the race relations situation appears in all its drama. The tragedy is somewhat tinged with humor but completely suffused with suffering.

The story as was mentioned is simple. The problem it describes, however, is exceedingly complicated. To understand it, let alone to solve it—if indeed there be a solution—requires much soul-searching as well as brain-wracking.

In this play the author suggests that the antagonism between Negro and white is already caught in the Biblical account of Cain's murder of Abel. At present, it is natural to identify the white man with the murderer, Cain. How much would it take to change the situation and have the Negro be the murdering one?

"The Blood Knot" declares that the bond of brotherhood in our day poses a kind of problem which is not only knotty, but bloody.

5'.

"Blues for Mr. Charlie"

Text: And He said unto him: "What is thy name?"
        And he said: "Jacob."
        And He said: "Thy name shall be called no more Jacob, but Israel; for thou hast striven with God and with men, and hast prevailed."
                                                        —Genesis 32:28, 29

In the area of American white-Negro relationships two imaginary names have become famous—Uncle Tom and Jim Crow. Now, James Baldwin has written a Broadway play which would make a third fictional name, Mr. Charlie, also well-known.

In his first play, "Blues for Mr. Charlie", Mr. Baldwin presents him as the Southern Negro's conception of the white man. This view is a combination of feigned respect and restrained insurrection. As the title suggests, this figure of Mr. Charlie faces a sad ending, since the Negro revolt is mounting.

Not unexpectedly, Baldwin's play, with its strong language,

seethes as it unfolds. What may be considered to be remarkable is the large number of references to the Bible in this drama. One of these is the way in which the father, whose son has been murdered, mourns for him. His phrases are similar to King David's elegy for his son, Absalom.

Another striking instance of a Biblical overtone is the statement by one of the Negro characters, that like Jacob of old they should wrestle with man and God Himself, if need be.

The aggrieved determination of the Negroes to rid themselves of Mr. Charlie is presented especially forcefully in the final scene in which striking reference to the Bible is made. A copy of the Bible and a gun are placed together, to make the point that force will be utilized henceforth to achieve the Biblical ideals of racial equality and justice.

Only through violence, says the play, lies the end for Mr. Charlie. Let us pray that Mr. Charlie can disappear through the light of the Bible, with no recourse to violence.

If guns will have to be used, it may or may not sound the Blues for Mr. Charlie. It will surely bring thick darkness for all Americans.

3.   Kindness and Kinship

Great, great caution must be voiced and exercised against the counsel of violence as the way to achieve Brotherhood. Never let it be forgotten that the essence of brotherly love is kindness. Eugene O'Neill has expressed this idea beautifully in another connection.

"Marco Millions"

Text: It hath been told thee, O man, what is good,
And what the Lord requireth of thee:
Only to do justly, and to love mercy, and to walk
humbly with thy God.
                                        —Micah 6:8

Eugene O'Neill is regarded by many as America's greatest playwright. Not the greatest of his plays is "Marco Millions" which was selected by the Lincoln Repertory Theatre for presentation. The second best of O'Neill is still worthy of careful attention, for it is much better than most anything else.

"Marco Millions" is the story of Marco Polo given a fictional treatment by the dramatist. O'Neill uses the figure of the world traveler who reached the Orient from Venice to indicate the differences between the civilizations of the East and the West even in our own day.

More than just pointing to these differences, O'Neill maintains that the Western culture in comparison to that of the East is inferior, being devoid of spirituality. Marco, as the typical Westerner, is interested only in accumulating more and more financial wealth—"millions"!

Kukachin, an Oriental princess, refuses to believe that Marco, with whom she has fallen in love, is without a soul. "Because I have seen it," she says, "once when he bound up my dog's leg, once when he played with a slave's baby, once when he listened to music, and I heard him sigh. . ."

What Kukachin is saying is that kindness is the sign of a human soul. This is in part what Micah said: "What doth the Lord require of thee? But to do justice, to love mercy, and to walk humbly with thy God."

O'Neill may be right in claiming that Western civilization is unspiritual, but it is not because it does not have a tradition of spirituality. Hopefully, "Marco Millions" in repertory, in constant repetition, may help remind many through Broadway of the Bible that reflects our souls.

C. COURAGE

1. Don't Let Go

A man's character is a total of qualities and values—among which courage is a vital one. It requires courage to oppose evil and withstand the "slings and arrows of outrageous fortune". Dore Schary has given an interesting treatment of the virtue of courage.

"One by One"

Text: When thou shalt besiege a city a long time
         in making war against it, thou shalt not

destroy the trees thereof . . .
for thou mayest eat of them . . .
for is the tree of the field man, that it should be
besieged of thee?
Only the tree of which thou knowest that they are not
for food, them thou mayest destroy and cut down . . .
—Deuteronomy 20:19, 20

"Too many people waste their lives", exclaims the twenty-two
year old girl paraplegic who is determined not to be one of
these. She is the heroine of Dore Schary's new play, "One by
One".

Having fallen from a tree when she was a child of ten, she
has been paralyzed from her waist down since. The fall broke
her back, robbed her of the use of her legs, but it did not break
her spirit. Although she suffered much inner turmoil—frequently
when someone tried to help and shield her, she determined
to be as self sufficient as possible.

In her effort to be a whole person, Kathy even went further
than just taking care of herself, she found employment at a
rehabilitation institute where she helped other unfortunates
like herself to achieve a worthwhile life.

The words quoted from her at the outset of this piece she had
directed at a twenty-seven year old male paraplegic. He had lost
the use of his legs because of polio suffered four years earlier
while in the Army. Unlike Kathy, Jason cannot "take" his mis-
fortune and is in danger of disintegrating as a person.

To rouse him out of his crippled mental and spiritual attitude, Kathy utilizes her love for him to help him not only to
stand on his feet, but also to find joy in his love for her. In
this way, step by step, their lives are saved from being wasted.

The idea of not wasting precious human resources—even life
itself—has an interesting Biblical source. "Destroy no fruit-bear-
ing tree, even in warfare", says the Bible. On this basis, the
religious principle has developed that it is a sin to waste anything precious.

Perhaps plays like "One by One" can sensitize us to the sin
of such wastefulness, whatever the way we indulge in it. From
such sensitivity, hopefully may come healing. It is too bad that
the play did not last longer. Another waste!

2. The Aftermath of Insecurity

a. Personally

The cultivation of the quality of courage is essential for living ethically. When man is beset by a sense of insecurity, he may yield to temptation to act degradingly and evilly. This is true not only of an individual but of a whole nation as well. Consider this truth as it is revealed in a play (the individual, a.) and a moving picture (the nation, b.)

"A Murderer Among Us"

Text: And when the people saw that Moses delayed
to come down from the mount,
the people gathered themselves together under Aaron,
and said unto him, "Up, make as a god . . ."
—Exodus 32:1

And Moses said unto Aaron: "What did this people say unto thee, that thou hast brought a great sin upon them?"
And Aaron said: "Let us not the anger of my lord wax hot;
thou knowest the people, that they are set on evil."
—Exodus 32:21, 22

A devotee of the Hitchcock type of murder mystery will be delighted with "A Murderer Among Us", the newly arrived play at the Morosco Theatre. Although the famous director had nothing to do with it, the play has all the ingredients of a Hitchcock production, including suspense, a peculiar humor, and a surprise ending.

Truth to tell, upon second thought, a student of human nature, especially as this study is made in the light of the Bible, should not find the outcome so unexpected. Yves Jamiague, the playwright, makes some penetrating comments about the nature of society, and man's actions and reactions in it.

One of these observations concerns itself with the power of wealth. One of the characters who suddenly comes into possession of a great deal of cash, brandishes these bills and says in part: "Now, I want, I order, I demand!"

Another astute comment by the author which may be regarded as the main point he makes, is that because of fear, people will do most anything unjust.

This is what determines the final outcome of the play. As was already mentioned above, anyone familiar with the Bible, especially with its story of the Golden Calf, will not be surprised by the way the play ends.

In the case of that Biblical incident, it was the people's fear of what would become of them because of Moses' tarrying on Mount Sinai that led them to reveal their basic tendency to do evil. It is the same fact of fear that according to Jamiague, elicits not only a murderer among us but in us.

b. Nationally

"Seven Days in May"

Text: And when the people saw that Moses delayed
        to come down from the mount,
        the people gathered themselves unto Aaron,
        and said unto him: "Up, make us a god who shall
        go before us . . ."
                                                —Exodus 32.1

"Seven Days in May" is a current motion picture version of the recent best-selling novel of the same name. As such, the movie is most exciting and directly challenging to all Americans, although fortunately fictional.

Its story deals with a plot hatched by some members of the American Military High Command to take over the government of the United States. The chief plotter who would become the American Dictator is a general, brilliantly portrayed by Burt Lancaster. He believes that such a military coup is necessary in order to save America from its civilian leaders who favor an atomic bomb ban treaty with Russia.

The picture shows the seriousness of such a military threat. We would do well to ponder the thought expressed by the President (Frederick March) explaining why such a thing could happen. He explains that even Americans would accept a dictator because the times are so fraught with danger and uncertainty. Dismayed by the fearfulness of these days, they would avidly, albeit mistakenly, turn to anyone who would assure them safety and security.

The Bible records a similar occurrence. When the Israelites became frightened in the wilderness because Moses tarried on Mount Sinai, they insisted that Aaron make for them an idol. It was a Golden Calf which they had worshipped in Egypt, and which they believed would save them in their new dangerous environment.

Thus we see that what "Seven Days in May" gives today as a fictional analysis of a people's debacle in the face of insecurity, the Biblical account a long time ago has given as the God's honest truth.

3. The Source of Courage

True courage is not easy to come by. Faith in God, as a Power who manifests Himself in moral law, can help engender courageous action. An interesting fictional account of a number of Medal of Honor winners deals with the question of the sources of courage.

"They Came to Cordura"

Text: Only be thou strong and very courageous that thou
        mayest observe and do according to the teachings
        of Moses.
                                                —Joshua 1:7

Joshua fought the Battle of Jericho—and he had something important to say about courage. This intrepid Hebrew leader knew courage at first hand. He had seen it operate in others and in himself. He had observed the Hebrew slaves whose slavishness made them unfit for deeds of heroism. He knew the courage required to be one of the twelve scouts sent into Canaan to report about the land and its inhabitants. He knew the even greater courage required to stand with Caleb against the ten other scouts differing with the majority's report. The Bible tells us that of all that generation which left Egypt only Joshua and Caleb were privileged to enter the Promised Land.

In the light of the above, the motion picture, "They Came to Cordura", becomes more meaningful. Its foreword informs

the viewers that Glendon Swarthout, whose book was used as
the basis of the film, had been interested in expounding the
anatomy of courage.
The picture shows the efforts of a U.S. Army major during
the Mexican War to lead through dangerous country to Cordura, a town behind the lines, a contingent of five nominees for
the Congressional Medal of Honor. Throughout the film, various questions are raised concerning the nature of courage.
What causes cowardice? Are the springs of courage necessarily
noble? How deep does fearlessness lie? What is the highest de-
gree of courage?
Some things become clear as the picture comes to its end.
True religion requires courage to face the slings and arrows
of outrageous fortune, to offset man's inhumanity to man, and
to still the enemies within one's own soul.
Yes, to get to the Cordura of every man's salvation produces
big action and requires even *bigger faith.*

4. Heroes

Men sometimes learn to be courageous by taking example
from others. In the future history of mankind the exploits of
the Warsaw Ghetto—dramatized in play form as well as it was
in literature—will serve as inspiration.

"The Wall"

Text: And Samson said, "Let me die with the Philistines."
—Judges 16:30

Almost everyone knows the story of Samson. We remember
the Bible's account of how in a weakened condition this famous
strong man was captured by the enemies of his people. Later,
when he regained his strength, he uprooted two pillars upon
which the Philistine's temple rested. This brought the roof
crashing down upon him and his oppressors. He knew that by
doing this, he would die. He also knew that many Philistines
would be brought to death through his act of suicide. Samson
was satisfied that his death at least would prove costly to his

enemies. His act of heroism has become a classic example of man's courage and indomitable spirit in the face of insuperable odds.

Recent history has produced another such example. The Jews of the Warsaw Ghetto finally determined in the dark days of the Second World War not to die cheaply. They fought with practically no arms against Hitler's Wehrmacht. Naturally they were destroyed. Nevertheless, their deaths proved costly to a number of the enemy who paid for their cruelty with their own lives.

This heroic stand has been described in John Hersey's prize novel, "The Wall". Millard Lampel wrote a play based on the book.

This play was produced two seasons ago on Broadway. Theatre goers stayed away in droves because they feared the story might prove morbid.

Quite the contrary. It should have been viewed as a story of group heroism more than equal to the individual heroics of a Samson.

D.   INDIVIDUAL RESPONSIBILITY

1.   Man Made in the Image

A certain type of religious person, in his determination to do what is right, is fearless. He feels that his interest in life goes beyond himself. Therefore, he is ready to put his life in jeopardy, if necessary. This only emphasizes, however, his high regard for his own individuality, for his share of responsibility for the better life.

Even if one, like the hero of Lorraine Hansberry's last play, does not profess a belief in God as the reason for his sense of moral responsibility by his deeds, he acts as if he has such faith.

"The Sign in Sidney Brustein's Window"

Text: And God created man in His own image . . .
—Genesis 1:27

Sidney Brustein, the hero of Lorraine Hansberry's play currently on Broadway, has a sign on his window. The window is in his ground floor, practically basement, apartment in Greenwich Village. Being thus easily seen from the street, the sign calls for the election of a certain political candidate.

The play entitled "The Sign in Sidney Brustein's Window", as now presented, has not been polished completely by its authoress. This is so because unfortunately Miss Hansberry, gravely ill, did not have a chance to finish her work.

For all of this, the play is sufficiently advanced to move audiences in a penetrating fashion. The story revolves around Sidney, his wife, his two sisters-in-law, an upstairs white neighbor, and a friend who is a Negro. Each of these has a heavy set of personal problems to bear.

So crushing is the load that one of the sisters-in-law commits suicide. All the others react to their situations in various ways. At the end, Sidney realizes that Reform solicited by his sign is more than a matter of electing political candidates. It is something much deeper, touching every individual's character, and desperately needed in our particular stage in history.

What Miss Hansberry sees in Sidney Brustein's sign is something of that which the late President Kennedy meant when he said: "Ask what you can do for your country". It is of a piece with the ancient Biblical tradition which recognizes the role of the individual as central to the improvement of society and to his own fulfillment.

The Bible, it has been noted, in reporting the creation of the creatures of the universe, mentions that mankind is the only species that was created from an individual. The Biblical standard of individual moral responsibility is more than the sign in Sidney Brustein's window. It is the unchanging sign for all time.

2. The Yes and No of Conformity

Since living as a person is so complex, it should not be surprising that man's desired independence sometimes must be tempered by a willingness to conform with society. Modern society, however, for all of its non-conformists, has been diagnosed as suffering from too much conformism. The proper attitude to conformism which is needed at times is the burden of a play which starred Jason Robards on Broadway.

"A Thousand Clowns"

Text: He declareth His words unto Jacob,
        His statutes and His laws unto Israel.

                                              —Psalms 147:19

From a clown you expect entertainment. From "A Thousand Clowns," a play thus titled you may receive entertainment and more. This "more" is an impetus to think about such serious matters as freedom, conformity, the human personality, and even the nature of the Divine.

The hero of "A Thousand Clowns", the recent Broadway hit, now showing at the Paper Mill Playhouse is a noncomformist, Murray Burns. A television writer who has been creating a children's program featuring Chuckles the Chipmunk, he rebels against the stupidities and inanities he is producing and quits. His failure to have a job might not be such a serious problem except for the fact that his eleven year old nephew, Nick, who lives with him has come to the attention of a social work agency.

To keep Nick in his home he must get back to work, which means continuing to write the very material he resents. In the course of developments he meets and falls in love with Sandra, a social worker. The latter revels in the new-found freedom she enjoys in Murray's non-conformist way of life. Soon though, she realizes, as Murray slowly comes around to the realization too, that non-conformism, even as conformism, is bad when practiced to an extreme.

There is something attractive in Murray's assertion to Sandra that every human being should be like "the little red car in the circus which putters around, suddenly its doors open and out come a thousand clowns, whooping and hollering. . ." We find charming Murray's report of his associate's conception of God to the effect that "he is really a fine guy".

Maturer thinking would have us appreciate, however, that while we all want to express ourselves freely, and while we would want to picture God as rejoicing in His universe, the way of the world calls for freedom only under Divine laws and within social customs. Without such a balance between conformity and non-conformity, the meaning of God and man and society would disappear.

Not a single clown, nor a thousand clowns, can disprove this fundamental aspect of life.

E. TRUTH-LOVING AND TRUTH-SEEKING

1. Keeping a Vow

For anyone seeking to understand the nature of man, and to appreciate the values by which he lives, the idea and ideal of truth are very much involved. How does man arrive at truth? Can he be depended upon to tell the truth? What is truth? These are questions which cut across the dual nature of man— his bestial quality wherein trickery and ensnaring are expected, and his spiritual character wherein honesty and integrity are the norms.

Based on an unlikely legend centuries old, a Hebrew play has become a classic as it stresses the importance of keeping one's word as a mark of humanity.

"The Dybbuk"

Text: Better it is that thou shouldst not vow
       than thou shouldst vow and not pay.
                                          —Ecclesiastes 5:4

"The Dybbuk" is world famous as a classic Hebrew play. Written originally in Russian by S. Anski, it was translated into beautiful Hebrew by C.N. Bialik. What is now the National Theatre of Israel, Habimah, has presented this play more than two thousand times.

In its Yiddish translation, as well as in its Hebrew, it has come to be accepted, not only among Jews, but among all peoples as one of the outstanding dramas of the world.

Generally it is known to be a spiritualistic play. Dealing with a heroine who is possessed by the spirit of her dead lover, the play depicts the efforts of her Jewish coreligionists to exorcise that spirit called in Hebrew a "Dybbuk".

What may be missed in all of the drama of these developments is the unbelievably strong ethical principle which is the basis of the play. The story has it that two friends who are prospective fathers vowed that should they have children of

opposite sex, they would join them in marriage. A daughter
and a son are born to each respectively. The son's father dies.
The girl's father becomes wealthy with the passing of time.
When the date for the girl's betrothal arrives, her father for-
sakes his vow made before her birth.

It is this forgotten and broken vow that gives rise to the
tragedy with its spiritual upheavals. The Bible maintains that
Heaven and Earth are shaken when a solemn promise is broken.
This Biblical attitude to the sanctity of a pledged word has
remained so firmly implanted in the consciousness of the people
of the Book that a story like that of "The Dybbuk" could be
developed among them.

It may well be that in our own day "The Dybbuk's" theme
would not appear so fanciful, if the sense of sanctity of one's
pledged word were more a fact.

2. Slander and Libel

Man's inhumanity to man does not appear only in the acts
he commits against his fellowman, but also in the words he lets
loose as poisoned arrows against his fellows. The autobiography
of Louis Nizer, the famed attorney, furnished a plot for a fine
play dealing with this aspect of human villainy.

"A Case of Libel"

Text: Thou shalt not go up and down as a talebearer
        among thy people; neither shalt thou stand idly by
        the blood of thy neighbor: I am the Lord.
                                            —Leviticus 19:16

Slander and libel are regarded in the Biblical tradition as
among the most pernicious of sins. Character assassination is not
only morally injurious to the one defamed, but also to the
slanderer himself. Moreover, even those who receive the slanderous or libellous material are damaged spiritually.

The Bible, therefore, urges that each person stand on guard
against slander. Because of its nature, however, a slander is very
difficult to handle. First, the argument can be advanced that
every man has a right to express an opinion—even a wrong one.
Another difficulty is that in dealing with a libel, one must re-

peat it. The very repetition then spreads the defamation! Furthermore, the protagonist for the libelled is immediately put on the defensive himself for associating with such an accused. For all these reasons, and more, people tend to do nothing when a slanderous remark reaches them. The Bible speaks out against this "tendency": "Thou shalt not stand idly by the blood of thy neighbor."

The forceful drama, "A Case of Libel", a Broadway coproduction of Roger Stevens and Joel Schenker portrays the human characteristics involved, even as the Bible suggested, in a situation where a libel has been committed. Starring Van Heflin, Sidney Blackmer and Larry Gates, the play is based on the famous Reynolds-Pegler libel case in which Louis Nizer was the attorney for the plaintiff.

In developing the idea that every man has the duty to nail the lie to a libel, the play by Albert Denker based on Nizer's "My Life in Court", uses the techniques of the theatre admirably. This is "A Case of Libel" which should be talked about and spread abroad widely.

3.   Middle Age—the Untrustworthy Age?

In the maze of unreality, falsehood and deception that is in the nature of man and his civilization, there is need for a standard of Truth. Such a standard is the Bible. An indirect and unfounded criticism of part of it may be found in one of Thornton Wilder's works.

"The Matchmaker"

Text: The Song of Songs, Proverbs, Ecclesiastes.

Thornton Wilder's play, "The Matchmaker", was given a movie version some few years back. Now this film is enjoying a re-release. The reason for the reappearance of the film is undoubtedly the fact that the current musical comedy success, "Hello Dolly", is also based on the same Wilder play.

Even without the hit musical comedy's presence on Broadway, the moving picture of "The Matchmaker" is worthy of having a rerun. It is extremely well-acted as well as having some unusually interesting facets. Congratulations are never too late for Shirley Booth, Anthony Perkins, Shirley MacLaine and Paul Ford for their histrionics.

Special recognition should be given to the movie because of the strange way in which the actors occasionally speak directly to the audience, focusing attention on the fact that they realize that the story is just a story, but one with a moral.

At the end of the moving picture each of the main players gives his or her version of what the story teaches. In the course of the film, one of the comments made may also be considered as a lesson of the story because of its great depth of meaning. "The young are smart, as are the old. It's in between, in the middle years, that people get into trouble". In this connection one is reminded of the tradition that teaches that King Solomon, reputed to be the wisest of all men, wrote three books of the Bible. The Book of the Song of Songs, with its theme of love, when he was a young man. The Book of Proverbs with its practical wisdom, when he was middle-aged. Finally, the Book of Ecclesiastes with its message of pessimism when he was aged.

According to Wilder's character, "The Book of Proverbs" is not as wise as "The Song of Songs" and "Ecclesiastes". One does not have to be a Biblical scholar to disagree with that opinion. After all, that was just one person's opinion—and a fictional one, at that.

F. JUSTICE AND MERCY

1. The Quality of Justice

It goes without saying that the idea of justice must be accepted as a basic principle of proper human relations. Just what is the standard of justice has been the subject of many tomes of philosophic and legal theorizing. A charming motion picture had something significant to say about this subject recently.

"The Chalk Garden"

Text: What doth the Lord require of thee but to do justice, to love mercy and to walk humbly with thy God.
—Micah 6:8

A chalk garden is one where plants can not grow because the chalkiness of the soil dooms it to being unfruitful. The title of the current movie, originally a play with the same title, "The Chalk Garden", is meant to convey the thought that the household which is featured is symbolized by its unproductive garden. The story tells of a grandmother who has rejected coldly her widowed daughter for marrying again. The older lady also tries to alienate her daughter's daughter from her remarried mother. Because of this, the granddaughter suffers severe emotional and psychological disturbances.

The child—a teenager—is given to lying, to setting fires, and to acting as an imp generally. To handle her, a governess is engaged by the grandmother.

Court proceedings are instituted by the mother to secure custody of the child. The Judge has the occasion to remark that justice can not be concerned with pity, or with a consideration of motives and causes. Such matters, he declares, belong in God's province, not in that of a human judge.

To this the governess responds from bitter experience in her own life that where justice and mercy are not joined together, as practically a part of each other, there is no justice, no mercy and no true religion.

Here we may discover a beautiful and meaningful interpretation of the prophet Micah's three-fold dictum concerning man's duty to love mercy, to practice justice and to walk humbly with God.

All three must be so integrally related to each other that they are practically the one and the same thing. When these elements are so combined in the soil of human relations, then beautiful deeds and sentiments may blossom.

2. Equal before the Law

One of the basic assumptions of justice is that all men are equal before the law, however they may differ in status, ability and wealth. All men must be treated equally in the matter of justice. A shocking case of murder elicited from Clarence Darrow, the defense attorney, a brilliant exposition of this aspect of the human phenomenon.

"Compulsion"

Text: Ye shall do no unrighteousness in judgment;
        thou shalt not respect the person of the poor,
        nor favour the person of the mighty;
        but in righteousness shalt thou judge thy neighbor.
                                            —Leviticus 19:15

In a matter of justice, rich and poor must be treated equally. Such is the Biblical injunction. Knowing that the rich could influence judgment by bribes and other means, the Bible repeatedly warns against such perversion of justice by the rich.

The Bible also realizes that the poor just by reason of poverty might cause judges to "bend backward", causing justice to be perverted. Against such tendencies the Bible taught: "Thou shalt not overly respect the person of the poor, nor favour the person of the mighty." Both rich and poor must be equal before the law.

The interesting twist to the above maxim was provided in the twenties in the famous Leopold-Loeb murder case of Chicago. This twist is referred to in the movie, "Compulsion" which is based on that case. The lawyer in the film enacting the role of Clarence Darrow, the famous defense attorney, declares that the boys cannot find justice because they are rich. If they came from poor families, he argues, society would not be so bent on killing them for their senseless, youthful crime.

Here was a case where wealth prejudiced the boys to a harsher sentence than would have been meted out were they poor.

Not at all strange, but completely ironic is the fact that Clarence Darrow should be pleading against such a particular miscarriage of justice. To say the least, Darrow was not famous for his attachment to the Bible. Still, he found himself at one of the crowning moments of his career, pleading the ancient Biblical cause: "Ye shall do no unrighteousness in judgment". Rich and poor are to be treated alike in matters of justice— neither one, better or worse.

V

Pastime as Recreation

Time To Spend

In the preceding chapters we have considered the general question, "How do the values and directives for living as portrayed in the contemporary theatre shape up with the Bible's ideals in the areas of man's family life, education, economic and social endeavors?". The next step we propose to take is to consider the nature of drama as an art form, examined from the point of view of the Bible. Stated in the most general way, the aim of the theatre is to be a pastime. Since the Bible is intent upon enabling its adherents to spend their time—the essence of life (even as there can be no play without the passage of time)— properly, it is natural that there be a relationship between religion and the theatre.

Many have already written that in Man's development his first place of worship was his first theatre. The history of the development of the drama in the western world is replete with references to the different kinds of relationship between the church (and the synagogue to a far less extent) and the theatre through the centuries. The purpose of this chapter is to set forth some further relationships between the theatre as an art, and the Bible as a special compendium of the religious outlook.

The reader is reminded of the line by Shakespeare to the effect that "all the world's a stage". In this succinct statement is the suggestion that a good deal of the wisdom concerning the nature of man's life is caught in the character of that most human of all the manifestations of art—the dramatic. The thing to notice is how often and strikingly a permanent and fundamental value of life is revealed as an underlying principle for

the theatre art. Certainly, the recreational and leisure time pursuits called drama are of supreme value for the individual and social life.

The Bible is both concerned and involved in many ways with the theatre. The selections in this chapter present some of the meaning of the dramatic pastime—both as a way of the theatre and a way of the spirit.

A. SUBJECT FOR ENTERTAINMENT—THE BIBLE

In the early history of the theatre (church related always) in the western world, the Bible with its message was the main, if not only, subject for the playwrights. Since medieval drama originated in the church, the ritual, when given dramatic form, as in the dedication of a new church edifice, was Bible-centered. Miracle plays like "Daniel", the York plays, and morality plays such as "Everyman" are familiar examples of the use of the Biblical material.

When the secular theatre was born in the sixteenth century, the drama became a pastime "for pleasure more than for serious or religious responsibility". The Bible became less directly the subject for plays. Still, great plays with profound meaning had perforce to involve Biblical concepts in one way or another. The search for truth, the understanding of good and evil, and the need for redemption are for the western man always Bible-oriented, no matter how they may be treated and even how they may be handled with new insights.

The fact is though, that during the last generation few Biblical heroes and situations have been the direct subject matter for legitimate Broadway productions. During the last five years, "Gideon" was the one play with a Biblical hero.

Of course there have been innumerable Biblical references—both directly and indirectly—in our modern theatre. An interesting example of how an old Biblical joke, although not identified as such, is bringing laughs today, is to be found in a long-running comedy.

"Never Too Late"

Text: And Sara said: "God hath made laughter for me; everyone that heareth will laugh on account of me".
—Genesis 21:6

Studies having been made, a conclusion has been forthcoming that in human culture there is really just a limited number of basic ideas. In the field of music, for example, while variations on them may be countless, the main musical phrases are comparatively few.

The same is true in novel as well as play writing. Surprisingly small is the number of basic story plots. Whatever developments may be given them, the core plots are not many at all.

Along the same line, students of humor have discovered that jokes and humorous situations are derived from a few basic psychological ideas. Without delving into what these are, it is sufficient here to point to the fact that some jokes have become typed. The "mother-in-law" joke is a case in point.

Still currently on Broadway—it has been a smash success for three years—the play, "Never Too Late" is based on an experience which for all its seriousness has come to be regarded rightly or wrongly as funny. It is the situation where a middle-aged wife discovers that she is going to have a baby, long after she thought her child-bearing days were over! What happens to her, her married daughter, her son-in-law, and most especially her husband, furnishes the humorous material of "Never Too Late".

Although, of course, in a much different vein, this matter of late motherhood has been seen to be a subject for laughter way back in Bible days. Sara, in spite of her advanced years, found that she was going to bear a child. Not only she but her husband Abraham, were prompted to laugh. Indeed, the child when he was born was named "Isaac", which in the original Hebrew means "laughter".

As was mentioned above, the basic ideas for humor are few. The developments are varied and many.

B.   MOVIES DO MOVE

1.   Affecting Our Morals

More and more we should realize that drama has it in it to show meaning and purposes in life which stem from the Biblical revelation of man's highest values as well as his basic motivations. The motion picture in some ways can do this even more effectively than other forms of the theatre art. Having a special hold on the audience, the movie must therefore remember its special responsibility.

"Topkapi"

Text: Thou shalt not steal.

—Exodus 20:13

Do crooks always get caught finally? According to the movies, they do. In real life, of course, only too often they do not. Even though movies may be expected occasionally to present life situations truly as they are, it is right that they not show evil as ultimately triumphant. The reason? The particular nature of movies. They have an unusual way of having a tremendous imitative effect on viewers who tend to identify with the characters in films. Showing that crime might pay would encourage too many, especially the younger element, to get in on a similar payoff. Right living has a difficult enough road to travel without adding to its difficulties through the shimmerings of the silver screen.

These thoughts come to mind upon viewing a most enjoyable movie with an exotic title, "Topkapi". It is delightfully filmed in magnificent colors which appear as refractions of light from jewels. Jewels, indeed, figure prominently in the picture's story.

The Turkish National Museum holds some of the world's costliest jewels in a particularly well-guarded section called "Topkapi". It is this area which serves as the main locale of the action.

The film depicts the efforts of a band of jewel thieves, most of whom are amateurs, to steal a jeweled dagger out of this place. They are an engaging group who win the sympathy of the audience by their charm, their ingenuity and daring.

They are so attractive that one must suppress consciously the wish that they succeed in outwitting the Turkish police and achieve their illegitimate aim. It does not require much thinking to realize that this would be contrary to one of life's basic principles—"Thou shalt not steal".

No matter how charming the actors, how alluring the coloration of the prize, the movie "Topkapi" maintains that the

brightest jewels in the crown of civilization are still the Ten
Commandments. All movies are right in guarding them.

2. Magnifying Our Vision

The moving picture medium possesses techniques which are
not only especially impressive, but also inspiring. All "live"
shows—even religious Mystery Plays—are dwarfed by the po-
tentialities of modern movies for certain types of inspiration.

"The Windjammer"

Text: Bless the Lord, my soul! Lord, my God, Thou art
        very great . . .
      Thou wrappest Thyself in light as in a garment;
      Thou spreadest the heavens like a curtain.
      Thou buildest Thy upper chambers on the waters;
      Thou makest clouds Thy chariot, and ridest on the
        wings of the wind.
                         —Psalms 104:1–3

Cinerama is moving pictures, only more so. If the quality of
a motion picture is to approximate the nature of reality, then
Cinerama is the finest expression of this form of art. With color
and sound effects added, the Cinerama technique gives the
viewing audience such a sense of immediacy and naturalness
as to make the viewers actual participants in the action and
scenery projected on the screen.

An excellent example of this type of motion picture production is the recently reissued "The Windjammer". The title
refers to the sailing ship utilized for training young Danish
naval cadets who set out on a long cruise to various ports of
call. The pictorial description of their training and their experiences on land and sea affords a marvelous view of the over-
whelming power, beauty and glory of the forces of nature. In
addition, there is presented an intriguing display of some of
mankind's variegated cultural developments in art, music and
dance, as well as in architectural and mechanical feats.

Although the final scene of the film tells of a similar German
training sailing ship which has foundered with a loss of its
youthful crew—a report that raises questions about the reason-

ableness of such a universe—the overall effect of "The Wind-jammer" is to celebrate God's glory as seen in His world.

It is to the credit of Cinerama that it makes more evident what is so obvious all about us. Because the obvious we often tend to overlook, we may turn to a production such as "The Windjammer" to remind us of the Psalmist's declaration: "How manifold are Thy works, O Lord!"

C. BROADWAY, OFF-BROADWAY AND THE GENERAL NEIGHBORHOOD

While the movies have some technical advantages, creativity is not, for this reason, in them, any more than in the "live" stage. It is generally known that the off-Broadway theatre is where the more creative—in the sense of the more off-the-beaten path type of theatre—is presented. Recently, the off-off-Broadway has been added. In addition, the Metropolitan area around New York City has been enriched with a number of suburban thea-tres where some tryouts, and even experimental shows, have been produced.

Not as the best example of this type of play—it was a tryout for Broadway which it never reached—but rather to make a point of how the Bible may be utilized to enrich and broaden one's view of plays, we may consider a play that was shown in New York suburbia. This play is frankly not meant for the intellectual or the high-brow, but for just the ordinary theatre-goer who only cares to get some fun out of his theatre-going and may get it with something more.

"Thursday is a Good Night"

Text: This is the Lord's doing;
        It is marvelous in our eyes.
        This is the day which the Lord hath made;
        We will rejoice and be glad in it.
                                            —Psalms 118:23, 24

Do I think that Abe Einhorn and Donald Segall, the authors of the oh so light comedy, "Thursday is a Good Night", had any Biblical references in mind when they wrote this play? Of course I do not.

Do I propose that the co-authors of this play about a bookie and his special night-off activities and philanderings had any serious message to impart? Just as certainly is my answer here also "No".

Since my answers to these two questions are in the negative, do I feel myself justified to find any message of the spirit in connection with this obviously unserious offering? Here the answer is "Yes"—for the following reason.

Admittedly, it is wrong to read ideas into a play or any other work of art where these ideas cannot properly be read out. Such an interpretation would be tortuous and forced and unfounded. On the other hand if a frank recognition is made that the comment on a particular subject is only an idea that has been suggested through mere association of a phrase or word or an event, then such an interpretation is justified.

An example of this may be brought from "Thursday is a Good Night", recently performed at the Playhouse on the Mall, Paramus. In the play, the hero states that in reporting to the F.B.I. what had happened to him, it sounded so strange that even he could hardly believe it.

This statement may bring to mind the truth that our daily lives reflecting God's blessings which we accept as commonplace are upon reflection seen to be really wondrous experiences which should be "marvelous in our eyes".

Does the play, "Thursday is a Good Night", mean to teach this? No. Directly then there is no Bible in it. Since however, it suggests indirectly that every day and night are good and wondrous, then we may associate it with this Biblical concept. The Bible in this case though, must be viewed as not being actually on or even off-Broadway. It is only from the general neighborhood thereof.

D. A MOVIE OF THE ABSURD

The contemporary theatre has been described as having produced certain types of drama—the avant garde, and the theatre of the absurd, to mention but two. The latter is supposed to be difficult for popular consumption. An interesting and in many ways, exceptional case, of the theatre of the absurd was presented in a well-received movie.

"Dr. Strangelove"

Text: The heavens declare the glory of God,
        And the firmament showeth His handiwork . . .

                                                    —Psalms 19:1

        The law of the Lord is perfect, restoring the soul;
        The testimony of the Lord is sure, making wise the
        simple.

                                                    —ibid. 19:8

Until very recently, if they said that it couldn't be done, they would have been believed easily. Who would have imagined that one could utilize the motion picture screen to show a play that belongs to the Theatre of the Absurd? Moreover, who would have thought that such an effort could produce a box-office smash?

Yet this is precisely what happened with the moving picture, "Dr. Strangelove, Or How I Learned to Stop Worrying and Love The Bomb". Its very title—long and queer—at once suggests that here is a picture that is influenced by the so-called Theatre of the Absurd. It is indeed off-beat in treatment and in theme.

Such a theatre production has usually been associated with off-Broadway. Only rarely would one dare to think of producing such material on Broadway. That it should become a successful film is remarkable indeed, and should elicit our special attention.

The point of the film is that the present world with its two greatest nations linked through a "hot-line" to forestall its destruction is in an absurd situation. Moreover, mankind which is tinkering with its own perdition is acting absurdly.

The question may arise as if of itself. Are the foolishness and meaninglessness of humanity and the world today the essential nature of both?

The Bible would assure us that both mankind and the universe were planned by God to be other than absurdities. Both were meant to reflect the glory of God.

That the Theatre of the Absurd could come to the screen might have been hard to believe. It should have been even more difficult to imagine that human beings could have made themselves and their world so ridiculous. Unfortunately, it is not hard to believe because it is happening for all to see.

E. A TIME TO LAUGH

For the longest time, Aristotle's views of proper drama were accepted as normative. He has been regarded as the first and the greatest thinker dealing with the principles of the theatre art. Without at all saying that King Solomon should be regarded as expert as Aristotle in this regard, the simple fact is that the "wisest of men" did express some truths about life which apply as well to the field of drama. "To everything there is a season", said King Solomon, by which he meant that there is a time for everything. The peculiar power of drama is that of all the arts, it is the most human, and therefore the most interesting and attractive for people. Furthermore, it has the ability of conveying—"everything"—that "everything" for which in life there is a time. The following selections illustrate a number of different concerns of human life.

See first how a play can be made to satisfy man's need for fun.

"Enter Laughing"

Text: To every thing there is a season . . .
A time to weep, and a time to laugh . . .
—Ecclesiastes 3:1, 4

The Biblical book, Ecclesiastes, has come to be known as a book of pessimism. One of its recurring verses is: Everything is vanity.

Nevertheless, it has been accepted into the Canon because this pessimistic view of life is off-set by some other of its verses. One such is: The end of the matter, all having been heard: fear God, and keep His commandments. (Ch. 12 v. 13). Thus the pessimistic attitude is replaced by the religious view which sees life not sadly, nor even happily, but realistically.

In this realistic view of life, there is a time to weep and a time to laugh. The time of weeping is never avoided, for death is a constant. The time for laughing, however, has frequently to be sought.

How good therefore, to find on the current Broadway stage a play which brings laughter to audiences and audiences to laughter. The play, "Enter Laughing" boasts a splendid cast, all of whom excel in their respective roles. Each adds to the merriment.

Undoubtedly, there is a philosophy as well as a psychology of humor. The comedy of the Marx Brothers is a case in point. Surely, there is a Weltanschauung or psychological system implicit in the hilarity engendered for us by "Enter Laughing".

In our age of anxiety, in our time of tension, so great is our need for good fun, that most of us would be pleased just to know where to find it without bothering to analyze it.

Who would blame us? Surely not the Bible.

F. A TIME TO PLAY

A basic experience of man, from infancy through adulthood is play. L.P. Jacks, a famous British philosopher, has gone so far as to say that the ideal for man is where his work becomes play.

More than just accidentally the dramatic art form is called "play", and it explains much of its universal appeal.

"Easy Does It"

Text: To everything there is a season,
       and a time to every purpose under the heaven.
                                         —Ecclesiastes 3:1

At the Paper Mill Playhouse recently, and at the Yonkers Playhouse currently is being presented a jazzy comedy hit, "Easy Does It".

Starring Tom Poston and Elizabeth Allen, the story is about a public relations man's efforts to sell a detergent called "Easy".

The interesting thing about this theatre-piece is that it emphasizes, albeit innocently enough, a fundamental meaning of theatre itself. To the question "What is theatre?," "Easy Does It" offers a simple answer. Theatre fundamentally presents plays.

"What is a play?" may well be the next logical question in this connection. Without referring to the various aspects of it which may be considered in answering the question, there is no denying that a play is supposed to be just that—*play*. Indeed, the actors are called players and we speak of their roles as being played!

To see "Easy Does It" is to witness actors at play in a play. There is something in the human personality that responds to the urge to play. The Book of Ecclesiastes recognized the multifarious character of the human experience. "To everything there is a season. A time to be born, and a time to die; a time to break down, and a time to build up; a time to embrace, and a time to refrain from embracing; a time to keep silence and a time to speak; a time to love, and a time to hate."

Added to all these "times for" is the "time for play". As with all the other "seasons", so with the play season these are not at all lasting. Many a producer has discovered on Broadway what the Bible suggested a long time ago. Even the time for play depends on the changing human mood.

G. A TIME TO ANALYZE

Another play which did not "make it" to Broadway, "Days of the Dancing" had nevertheless something about it which makes it a fit example of the drama's great gifts—the ability to help audiences analyze the circumstances in which they live. In all of this, the Bible is a natural partner.

"Days of the Dancing"

Text: The joy of our heart is ceased;
        Our dance is turned into mourning.
                                                —Lamentations 5:15

Bravo! Just completed a pre-Broadway showing, at the Paper Mill Playhouse in Millburn is a play, that for its splendid effort to make contemporaneous the meaning of traditional religious ideas and terms, deserves our commendation. Its title is "Days of the Dancing".

John Bridges, the author, and the Actors Studio cast, headed by Shelley Winters and Robert Walker provide reason for satisfaction in each of us by showing that the present-day American theatre can go deep beneath surface sensationalism and provide food for thought.

Unfolding before us the story of a fallen woman, who is a fortune-teller of sorts, a palm-reader to be exact, the play deals essentially with her contact with a group of way-out teenagers who congregate in a neighborhood bar. One of these young men, sixteen years her junior, becomes her special interest and she, his.

Her relationship with him reveals that her previous unrequited love for someone led to her downfall. We also learn that the young man has been hurt similarly by an unfortunate love affair.

In the enactment of the play, interesting singing of and dancing to typical teenage music of our day are featured. This entertainment, however, does not drown out the unmistakable references to the Bible and its theology.

The technique employed for this is various. In one case, for example, a ditty is sung with the line: "So the Bible says: it is still true today." In other instances, there are direct Biblical citations, as when the palm-reader refers to her young friend as David arrayed against her Goliath to defend her honor.

Most interesting is the usage of a stage "word game" where words are presented to a character in the play for definition. These words include such as vengeance, redemption, the nether-world—all good theological terms.

It should be noted that these Biblical references in the play are used to analyze the current social malady—"our dancing is turned to mourning"—but not to prescribe the cure.

H. A TIME TO UNDERSTAND

Another way to express the unusual power of the drama for education is to say that plays help people understand. Plays accomplish this—more or less—depending on the artistry and skill of those who present them. Very well done, indeed, was a play dealing with the problem of aging.

"The Chinese Prime Minister"

Text: Your old men shall dream dreams;
        Your young men shall see visions.

                                        —Joel 3:1

Aging is becoming a more and more current subject. Since the years of an average person's life in our society are being extended, an older population is resulting with the matter of geriatrics coming to the fore. Senior citizen groups, also called golden age circles, are contemporary social phenomena which were unknown only two decades ago.

The immediacy of this whole subject of an aging population can explain in part the appearance on Broadway of the play, "The Chinese Prime Minister" which deals with this matter. Another part of the explanation for the play's presence on Broadway may be that the gifted authoress, Enid Bagnold, having herself passed the Biblical quota of three score and ten years, thought sensitively about the subject of aging and from her thinking brought forth this fine play.

The play by Miss Bagnold features as heroine an actress who is about to celebrate her seventieth birthday anniversary. Her two sons are having marital difficulties. Her butler is super-annuated and is on the brink of death. Her husband, whom she has not seen for many years, reappears.

With principally this cast of characters, Miss Bagnold has created her play that dazzles with wit and is brilliant with observations about life, especially in its aspect of a human being growing older.

For example, Margaret Leighton, who plays the leading figure splendidly, is given this line to say: "As beauty vanishes, the eyes grow dimmer. How good of God!" Also, she points out that the child is not the boy, nor the boy the man, nor the young man the old man. There are real differences.

Years ago, the prophet Joel said that the old men dream, while the young see visions. A dream is not exactly a vision. Even prophets see differently as they grow older. A prophet himself, Joel expressed this truth not only for his generation, but prophesied it for ours as well.

I. A TIME TO CONFIRM

Life calls for affirmations and confirmations. The latter becomes the case when we affirm that we know what we know.
One of the capacities of the theatre is to serve as an artistic in-
strument for confirmation of man's ideals.

"The Trojan Women"

Text: Through the window she looked forth, and peered,
       The mother of Sisera, through the lattice.
       Why is his chariot so long in coming? . . .
       The wisest of her princesses answer her . . .
       Are they not finding, are they not dividing the spoil?
       A damsel, two damsels to every man . . .
                                         —Judges 5:28–30

Euripides was more than a great Greek playwright. He was,
in addition, an excellent critic of the Greek people among whom
he lived and created. In this dual capacity of playwright and
critic, he became a shining inspiration for all mankind.

In "The Trojan Women" now being presented at the Circle
in the Square Theatre in New York City, Euripides expressed
in a play that deserved to become a classic his disapproval of
Greeks at war. Not only the heartlessness of the Trojan War,
especially brutal and bestial, but the bitterness of all war was
the object of his argument. Through his criticism of Greek
warfare, he offered a light for the world.

He afforded this light through the eyes of Trojan women,
as he presented them in his play. The terrible cruelties of war,
he pointed out, weigh especially heavily on women. They suffer
most the loss of loved ones. They remain alive with sorrowful
memories and aching servitude to victorious, murderous masters.

A similar stroke of artistic genius in describing the anguish
of war through the eyes of women is found in the Book of
Judges where Sisera's mother is pictured as watching and wait-
ing expectantly for the return from battle of her son, a Syrian
general. At that point she did not know that he had been slain.
What must be a sudden turn from happiness to grief for her
is left to the imagination.

Thus do the Biblical and the Greek literary artists utilize a

similar approach—the effect on women folk—to make their point
most dramatically about the viciousness of war. The Greeks had
the words for it, and so did the Hebrews. Now it is for the world
to pay attention to them.

J. A TIME TO PREACH

In its functioning as a reflection of a nation's culture, the
theatre for the Jews with their natural inclination for matters
spiritual, has become characteristically a pulpit.

"Habimah"

Text: And all the peoples shall walk, each in the name of
        its god, and we shall walk in the name of the Lord our
        God forever.

—Micah 4:5

George Bernard Shaw has declared the stage of the theatre
to be the world's greatest pulpit. This outstanding playwright,
philosopher and wit recognized that the theatre had a tremendous capacity to influence, to instruct, and to inspire.

Currently in New York City and Newark, and soon to appear in other American communities are the Israel National
Theatre actors, Habimah, who give emphasis to the Shavian
thesis about the stage as a kind of pulpit.

Their Hebrew name in itself has a significant lesson of the
spirit to teach in this regard. The word "Habimah" is now
accepted as full-fledged Hebrew meaning "stage". Interestingly,
the word is not found in the Bible. It is first used in the Tal-
mud which is post-Biblical. As such it is assumed to be of Greek
origin and to have been assimilated into Hebrew usage. So
complete has been the assimilation that it has come to mean
the pulpit in a synagogue. Thus the very name of the Israeli
National Theatre, Habimah, underscores George Bernard Shaw's
opinion of the stage as being a pulpit.

What may be said to be one of the basic spiritual ideas which
the world-famous Habimah spreads abroad?

Accepted as purely and authentically Hebraic, especially when
presenting such plays as their classic, "The Dybbuk", the Habimah players have incorporated and assimilated many non-Jewish

elements into their productions. The very staging and stylized acting of "The Dybbuk" which have become traditional with them, were the products of such non-Jewish mentors as Stanislavsky and Vachtangov.

The same is undoubtedly true of other national theatres in the world. Each has its own peculiar cultural character, while it has been influenced by others.

What, then, is one of the great sermonic texts taught by the world-famous Habimah, the stage which is as a pulpit? In the temple of art, as it should be recognized in the temple of life, each nation has something enriching to offer in the service of universal truth, goodness and beauty.

K. A TIME TO DESCRIBE

Another play which has been presented by the Habimah players reveals the peculiar power of drama to reconstruct experience.

"Children of the Shadows"

Text: The fruit of thy land, and all thy labors,
shall a nation which thou knowest not, eat up;
and thou shalt be only oppressed and crushed always;
so that thou shalt be mad for the sight of thine eyes
which thou shalt see.
                                             —Deut. 28:33, 34
Yea, though I walk through the valley of the shadow
of death, I will fear no evil, for Thou art with me . . .
                                             —Psalms 23:4

Habimah, the National Theatre of Israel, selected "Children of the Shadows" for its second play presented at the Little Theatre during its current tour of the United States.

The action of the play takes place at the seashore of Tel Aviv in the spring of 1956. The story concerns itself with Yoram who was brought to Israel from Poland by one of the agencies when he was fourteen years of age. Having grown up amongst Israeli youth, Yoram tries to deny his European tragedy-laden past, going so far as to declare himself a Sabra, a native born Israeli.

The past catches up with him, however, through several of

his relatives who recognize him. One of these, a Dr. Sigmund Rabinowitz, has special problems with his own past. Dr. Rabinowitz had been a collaborator with the Germans during the War. Because of the horrors he witnessed perpetrated against the Jews—horrors which he aided—the doctor has lost his mind, but not his intention ever to permit himself to forget or to forgive himself.

The frightful tragedies of the Nazi-tortured Jews understandably has led many of those who survived, young and old, to become emotionally and mentally disturbed, even unbalanced. These are the ones who are the "children of the shadows" of that dark disaster. Deuteronomy (chapter 28) already described well the human effects of such destruction.

To deal with these "shadows", and the "children" thereof, is a very present question of life and death. It is the question dealt with in the Habimah's second play on Broadway. Witnessing it, leads one to hope for the Psalmist's desideratum, "Yea, thought I walk through the Valley of the Shadow of Death, I shall fear no evil, for Thou art with me".

L. A TIME TO CONTEMPLATE

The theatre in its various manifestations has special human significance. Being most life-like of all the arts, it can convey truths about life by the very form in which it appears. Comedy, tragedy, farce, for example, reflects life's meanings; also, the very form of the theatre-medium such as the moving picture, pageant, or play may reflect a concept of the realities of life and death, worthy of contemplation.

The following are three examples of the above.

1. Immortality

"Marilyn"

Text: There the wicked cease from troubling,
        And there the weary are at rest.
        There the prisoners are at ease together;
        They hear not the voice of the taskmaster.

                                    —Job 3:17–19

Man naturally wants to know what is beyond the grave. In the course of the development of man's ideas about the possibility and nature of life after death, various concepts have been advanced. The writers of the Biblical books refer to some of these ideas as they made their appearance on man's spiritual horizon.

An interesting, albeit early, view of immortality is the Hebrew conception of Sheol, the nether world. Although the idea varies in Scriptures, the concept developed of a place where the departed from this earth continue to exist in a shadowy form. The author of Job, differently from other Biblical writers, describes Sheol as having advantages over this world. In that other world, the "weary are at rest", and the inequalities of mortal existence are set at naught.

Thoughts of immortality, and with them the ancient concept of Sheol, may come to mind as one views a screening of "Marilyn", a movie featuring the late Marilyn Monroe. Narrated by Rock Hudson, the film is a composite of scenes selected from Miss Monroe's earlier pictures, and from her last incomplete one.

Moving pictures—especially as talkies—have a strange quality about them when they present someone whom you know has died, yet appears to be alive, active, even singing and dancing before your eyes! In this case, the impression of strangeness is intensified because in tracing Miss Monroe's rise from bit parts to stardom, she appears in different roles.

"Marilyn" may lead one to wonder whether the film was not a kind of scientific approximation of the ancient Sheol-concept of a shadowy existence after death. Saddened by her untimely passing, still enjoying her gifts for entertaining, one may consider her famous initials, M.M., as standing for the compounded Mystery of life—here and hereafter.

2. Purpose of Living

"Stop the World—I Want to Get Off"

Text: And Job spoke and said:
        Let the day perish wherein I was born . . .

                                                        —Job 3:2

Then Job answered the Lord, and said:
"I know that Thou canst do everything."

—ibid. 42:1, 2

It was William Shakespeare who said that all the world's a stage, and men and women are players. There is much truth in this analogy.

Recently, Anthony Newley presented an aspect of this Shakespearian figure in his own play in which he pictures life as taking place under a carnival tent with the world as a kind of merry-go-round. Using the technique of pantomime, he calls his leading character "Littlechap", who lives through a life cycle on the stage.

Although Littlechap can hardly be considered a typical Britisher, (the play is set in England) he does reveal some familiar human traits common to all men. When in serious trouble, he cries with a whimper: "Stop the world (which is as a merry-go-round), I want to get off!"

It is with such a cry that he was born, as if declaring by it that he did not really want to be born. It is with a similar cry that he receives the harshest blows that hit him during his lifetime. Despite his outcry, the world of course, never stops. Somehow, though, he makes adjustments to his troubled existence.

The Bible, too, knows of such a human reaction of despair with life. Job, according to Scriptures, cried out in the days of his greatest troubles, "Cursed be the day on which I was born."

In the end, however, Job having lived an ethical life, becomes reconciled to his lot, and declares anew the Glory of God. Littlechap is not so fortunate, for he discovers finally that he has spent this life as a mere selfish existence. Because of this, in place of "Hallelujah", he can only sing finally: "What kind of fool am I?"

3. Life as Divine Comedy

"Seidman and Son"

Text: He that sitteth in heaven laugheth.

—Psalms 2:4

The Greeks and the Romans bequeathed classic plays to our western civilization. Not so the Hebrews. Yet the Bible reveals much dramatic power. The Holy Scriptures offer a dramatic interpretation of history. Viewing all of mankind's strivings as a divine drama, God is the Hero who together with his faithful followers must ultimately be victorious. His people, His prophets or His saints may suffer defeat from time to time, but the final victory belongs to God and to them who are loyal to Him.

This faith which holds that in the drama of real life, God the Hero emerges triumphant, makes human history a divine comedy. Our text from the Book of Psalms pictures God as not only achieving victory over the forces of evil that oppose Him but also as enjoying the spectacle as a play-goer might enjoy a play. Sitting in His High Place, God laughs at them who fight against Him.

An interesting example of comedy in the sense of a hero emerging triumphant in the end, is currently being exhibited in the Broadway production of "Seidman and Son", written by Elick Moll and featuring Sam Levene. Mr. Seidman has many problems to face. Among these are such as raising a teenaged daughter, coming to an understanding with his college-trained son who is to enter his father's dress business, labor troubles and marital difficulties. It is not that Mr. Seidman has an easy time of living that makes the story of his experiences as presented in the play a comedy. It is rather that in spite of everything, he comes through gallantly, humorously and well, that makes the play a comedy.

In every human being's life there are elements of tragedy. The Bible teaches and Mr. Seidman confirms that in the long run, righteous living—even as God Himself—emerges triumphant. In this fact of victorious living is the spirit of the comic drama of life in which we all have a part to play.

M. A TIME FOR TRAGEDY

Even though the Hebrews, unlike the Greeks for whom life was a tragedy, maintained that life was meant to be a comedy, they knew that there were many occasions of deepest tragedy in man's existence. The greatest playwright knew this also and expressed it.

"The Worlds of Shakespeare"

Text: . . . If harm befall him by the way in which ye go, then will ye bring down my gray hairs with sorrow to the grave .·. .

—Genesis 43:38

. . . Children I have reared and brought up, and they have rebelled against Me.

—Isaiah 1:2

The Bible is the Book of Books because it reflects life most truly. The human condition is best understood and described in it.

Dealing with tragedy which oft-times is an aspect of man's existence on earth, the Bible refers to various situations where it is experienced most bitterly. Among these is parental desolation brought about through children.

One of these instances mentioned in the Bible, deals with the suffering of a father who lives through his child's death. Jacob, who has lost Joseph, fears the tragic possibility of being bereft of Benjamin also.

Another case of parental dejection is given by the prophet Isaiah, who speaks of God as a Father who has seen his own children act treasonably against Him.

Suffering the loss of a child, and knowing rejection by a child, are cited by the Bible as sources of deepest tragedy for a parent.

It is interesting that Shakespeare—universally accepted as the greatest playwright in the English language—if not in any language—shows himself the master because of his understanding of human experience, including tragedy.

In his play, King Lear, Shakespeare presents an aged monarch's tragedy as compounded of treason against him by his two older daughters, and of the death of his youngest, faithful daughter while he is imprisoned.

Scenes from this and from others of his masterpieces have been presented recently at the Carnegie Recital Hall Theatre in a production entitled "The Worlds of Shakespeare" by Marchette Chute and Ernestine Perrie. Starring Vinie Burrows and

Earle Hyman with Lyn Ely and Norman Kean as producers, the performance was exemplary.

It emphasized Kierkegaard's view that a truly cultured person needs to know two things—the Bible and Shakespeare.

N. A TIME FOR GALLANT ADVENTURE

Whether comedy (as for the Hebrews), or tragedy (as for the Greeks), life has an additional appeal for all who can find it as a "gallant adventure". The American western highlights this quality.

"Gunfight at Comanche Creek"

Text: These are the statutes and the ordinances which ye
         shall observe to do in the land which the Lord
         has given thee to possess . . .
                                              —Deuteronomy 12:1

A "western" as a type of theatrical production is well-known not only to Americans but to people all over the world as well. As such, the "western" has come to reflect a recognizable format of acting, plot, action, scenery and cast of characters. In many ways, it reveals American mores and folkways.

The classic "western" features a taciturn, tall, handsome hero with a horse to match. Frequently, the hero is introduced as the stranger in town who immediately finds himself involved in battling the lawless elements in power. Quick on the trigger, an expert horseman, he is possessed of virtues which may be depended upon to achieve ultimate victory. It has been said that the typical western hero-cowboy would rather kiss his horse than the heroine. Lately, this aspect of the western has been undergoing changes.

In any case, there are some more aspects to the typical western which are beyond this brief treatment to describe. A good example of these, however, is to be found in the recently released film, "Gunfight at Comanche Creek", featuring Audie Murphy.

How explain the great popularity of the western? It is certainly dramatic and full of adventure. Surely, it is simple to follow as the "good guys" and "bad guys" struggle to the ultimate defeat of the latter.

One may speculate further that the underlying story of the western has a parallel in the Biblical account of how the Israelites were instructed to conduct themselves in conquering the strange, new territory of Canaan.

In this parallel resides a basic appeal to the human spirit to conquer with a frontiersman's courage the immoralities which bedevil society. It is this appeal which renders the western appealing, and the Bible sacred.

O. A TIME FOR CREATIVITY

The creative spirit of man is what lends him distinction and dignity. The life of the drama, as indeed the drama of life, calls out for it.

"She Loves Me"

Text: There is nothing new under the sun.

—Ecclesiastes 1:9

Frequently one hears repeated the famous statement attributed to King Solomon as reported in the Bible that there is nothing new under the sun. So much in life seems to confirm this opinion.

Political machinations and intrigue that may disturb a modern nation may be found to have been operative in ancient kingdoms. The difficulties that are experienced as our generation knows war and destruction may be seen to be similar to what was suffered thousands of years ago. Indeed, the examples may be multiplied manifold to give support to the notion that whatever is already was.

Further reflection reveals that although certain basic matters are constant in each era, there are changes and novelties that come into the world from time to time. The many inventions and discoveries, including the most recent explorations of space, are examples of this. In the world of art, similarly, there have been creative, new developments.

On Broadway at the present time are various types of theatrical productions. Each of these represents a development, something new in the history of the theatre.

For example, a most enjoyable musical, "She Loves Me", cannot be called properly a musical comedy. It is rather a play with music. The difference between such a play and a musical comedy (the musical comedy as a type of theatrical production is very recent) emphasizes that there is in fact something new under the sun.

Presenting the pessimistic view when declaring vanity of vanities, the Book of Ecclesiastes is prompted to declare that everything is always the same. In a different mood, Ecclesiastes would have recognized, perforce, the many changes which are part of the culture and civilization of mankind.

Thus, the Great White Way throws light on the moods as well as the truths of the Bible.

P. A TIME FOR LITERARY ART

How does man's creative urge express itself? We can say with certainty that it often appears as novel variations of an old literary form.

"The Theatre of Peretz"

Text: And he brought him forth abroad, and said:
       "Look now toward Heaven and count the stars,
       if thou be able to count them, and He said unto him,
       "So shall your seed be."
                                        —Genesis 15:5

The Bible may be studied from various points of view. To mention some—it may be considered as a repository of history, law, theology, ethics, as well as a work of literature. In this latter aspect, it may be pointed out that the Bible does some superb reporting. In many places, it features the type of writing known as realism. Also, by its very nature, it offers many instances of the genre of literary output described as romanticism.

One example of this is the beautiful promise divinely given to Abraham: "Thy seed shall be as the stars." Judah Leib Peretz, a truly great Yiddish and Hebrew writer—his short story, "Bontsche the Silent", is regarded as one of the world's classics —who wrote during the latter decades of the 19th and the first decade of the 20th centuries, has given this Biblical promise

an ironic turn. Yes, he wrote, the children of Israel are indeed
as the stars, being distant, scattered and separated from each
other! Much of Peretz' work has this character of ironic romanticism.

It is of interest to note that the modern theatre came into
being about the same time as Peretz functioned as a writer. The
cultural climate those days had an unmistakable air of ironic
romanticism, as well as realism. It is in such an atmosphere
that the modern theatre was born, and that Peretz wrote his
material.

Some of Peretz' stories have been dramatized and are now
being presented as an off-Broadway production. Peretz' view of
man, his relation to himself, to his neighbors and to reality is
an illuminating and charming reflection on theology and culture. "The Theatre of Peretz" reveals a remarkable relationship
between the ancient Bible and most modern off-Broadway.

Q. A TIME FOR HISTORY

Man's sense of history is one of the human differentia. The
theatre arts have a remarkable contribution to make in this
field. Two interesting examples from different media are "Cleopatra" and "Tovarich".

1. "Cleopatra"

Text: Babylon was a golden cup in the hand of the Lord . . .
                                              —Jeremiah 51:7

History is chronology with a corollary.

When the noting of dates and events in human experience
is set in order so as to derive meaning from them then "history"
is born. This addition, this corollary to chronology is the determining factor for the function of the historians.

Just what this factor is that renders events "historical" is determined by the historians themselves, all of whom have a
particular way of interpretation. Some, for example, are "economic determinists", believing that the driving force, and the
common denominator for all human endeavors is the urge for
economic benefit.

The writers of the Bible have arrived at a different corollary to human chronology. They may be said to be masters of "divine dialectics", for they see the hand of God in the unfolding of human history.

Since history, however conceived, is of vital moment to all intelligent people, a good question is "How to present the facts and issues of history most impressively?" Usually literature has been employed; witness Gibbons' "The Rise and Fall of the Roman Empire". Occasionally, with great success, the theatre art has been utilized; witness, Shakespeare's plays. More recently, within the present century in fact, the motion picture has shown itself to possess a special talent in this field.

Currently on Broadway is the most costly film ever produced, "Cleopatra". Featuring Elizabeth Taylor, Richard Burton and Rex Harrison, it has been conceived in great publicity over the personal exploits of two of its stars. Dedicated to the proposition that movie-goers the world over would be impressed by the opulence of Roman and Egyptian royalty, the movie uses abundantly the Hollywood technique to picture this.

For all of that, "Cleopatra" underscores the special merit of films to teach the nature of history, namely that history has more to it than just "his" and "hers"!

2. *"Tovarich"*

Text: "Therefore, fear thou not, O Jacob, My servant,"
        saith the Lord . . . "for lo I will save thee from afar,
        and thy seed from the land of their captivity."
                                              —Jeremiah 30:19

The Bible records the bitterly tragic occasion when the children of Israel knew captivity and exile at their worst. This followed upon the destruction of Jerusalem and the Solomonic Temple in 586 B.C.E. by the Babylonian King, Nebuchadnezzar.

Many of the people had been slain. A great number of the remainder were carried off as slaves to Babylonia. Some few escaped and became exiles in such distant lands as Africa, India and China.

Always, though, they had the hope expressed by their prophets such as Jeremiah that some day Jerusalem and its people would be reunited. This hope became their faith, and they lived by their faith.

Our century has become expert in recognizing different kinds of exiles. We hear of emigres, displaced persons, refugees. Presently on Broadway, an especially interesting and entertaining musical "Tovarich", featuring Vivien Leigh and Jean Pierre Aumont, deals with a particular group of emigres. They are White Russian aristocrats who fled the Bolshevicks. Not intended as a full-blown character study, this enjoyable play reveals insights into the traits and habits of these exiles living in Paris.

"Petersburg is not the burg it used to be. We must prove that we can sweep out, as well as sweep into a room". Thus a song in the play expresses their situation. They are aristocrats whose aristocracy is bankrupt. In order to live they must work, even at the most menial tasks. This situation they can accept with a certain humor.

Their exile, for all of that, is more complete than even that of the ancient Judeans. Who will prophecy for them a resurgence of the Czarist Russia they left behind?

R. A TIME TO ENNOBLE

In the history of the theatre itself one comes across different views as to the purpose of the stage. Is it to ennoble? Is it only to entertain? Some say today that the theatre is meant to reflect cruelty. When Kierkegaard said that a truly cultured person should know Shakespeare and the Bible, we think we know what kind of theatre he preferred.

Dore Schary

Text: The Book of Ezra

Most commonly the name of Ezra, the Biblical reformer of the fifth century, B.C.E. is followed by the title, "the Scribe". It is as Ezra the Scribe that he is known. It is as Ezra the Scribe that he enacted the reforms necessary in the Jewish life of his day.

Just what is meant by this appellation? The Hebrew word that is being translated as "scribe" is "sofer". It is being suggested that a "sofer" was not only one who wrote, i.e. acted as a scribe, but as in this case, was also a "bookman", a scholar of the Book, namely the Bible. The basis for this second meaning for "sofer" is the fact that the Hebrew word for "book" is "sefer". Hence, "sofer" is a scholar of the "sefer", the Book of Books.

It is significant that the Biblical tradition records the tremendous impact on the moral and social life of people exerted by "a sofer", a "scribe", a "scholar of the Bible". This is as it should be. Men and women have reason to expect from their literati and their artists and scholars, guidance and inspiration.

In none of the arts is there reason to expect more of such results than in the drama. One who writes for theatre deals not only with ideas and values, intellectually. He presents flesh and blood figures, the actors, in a dramatic way that can catch the conscience of the audience most grippingly.

It is good to know that among the contemporary playwrights there are those who like Dore Schary take seriously the privilege which is theirs to entertain, to enlighten, and to ennoble. Because the dramatist is engaged in the liveliest of all arts, and because he is formulating so much of that which is modern culture in a real sense, he is developing the Bible on Broadway.

S.   A TIME TO RECONSTRUCT

The role of the playwright in the reconstruction of society has been variously undertaken. Chekhov, the Russian doctor turned author, went about this in his own gifted fashion.

"The Chekhov Sketchbook"

Text: The Books of Ezra and Nehemiah

The Jews returned to Palestine from their exile in Babylonia some seventy years after their captivity of 586 B.C.E. Palestinian Jewish life did not recover quickly. It suffered from harsh economic conditions, from unfriendly neighbors, and from a lowering of spiritual standards.

The Biblical books of Ezra and Nehemiah relate how these two leaders arrived from Babylonia a generation or so after the Return to correct the unhappy situation in the Holy Land. Theirs was an activity of social reconstruction affecting the religious, familial, economic and communal life of their fellow Jews. During the last two seasons on and off-Broadway there have appeared revivals of several plays or adapted works of Anton Chekhov who faced a somewhat similar situation.

"The Chekhov Sketchbook" and "The Cherry Orchard" indicate unmistakably that Chekhov has something to tell us about the need for, and emergence of social reconstruction in Czarist Russia.

Unlike Ezra and Nehemiah, Chekhov, a doctor by profession, did not have the power to enact legislation to correct conditions. Nor did he offer a worked-out solution to the problems of human society. His was rather the artist's role of describing with tremendous understanding, humor, pathos and compassion the way life and light were faced together in the Russia he knew and among the Russians he loved. If in addition to this, a completion to a plan for rehabilitation is necessary for complete wisdom, then we must say that Chekhov had only the beginning of wisdom.

But even such beginning of wisdom bespeaks the fear of the Lord.

T. A TIME FOR PSYCHOLOGICAL DRAMA

A discussion of the dramatic art form with its special appeal for men and women might well include the fact that since man's mind (his psychology) is the human mark, the psychological drama figures prominently in a history of the theatre.

Here the point might be made that while the Bible is remarkable for the number of ways it is involved with drama, it would be wrong to expect to find in the Scriptures all forms of it fully developed. Although suggestive of some aspects of the theatre as an artistic and cultural experience, the Bible is necessarily limited.

"The Affair"

Text: And all Israel heard of the judgment which the king
       had judged; and they feared the king; for they saw
       that the wisdom of God was in him to do justice.
                                                    —I Kings 3:28

The Biblical book, I Kings, contains the story of Solomon.
It is a narrative that is replete with drama and human psychology.

A particularly interesting instance of this combination of
dramatic power and psychological insight is the account of the
two women who came for judgment by King Solomon. Each
claimed to be the mother of a particular infant. "And the
King said: 'Fetch me a sword. Divide the living child in two,
and give the half to the one, and half to the other." One woman
agreed to this, while the other demurred, saying, 'Let the child
live even if I do not have it.' "

It was the latter who Solomon decided must be the true
mother. Then, all Israel, as our text says, was impressed with
both the royal wisdom, and capacity for meting out justice.

This is a striking example from the Bible of drama and psychology as encountered in the pursuit of justice.

Yet it is not, properly speaking, psychological drama. This
would require a fuller treatment such as one finds in the dram-
atization of C.P. Snow's novel, "The Affair". This play which
appeared this season on Broadway is a psychological drama
concerning the achievement of justice.

Although the locale is an English college and the plot deals
with academicians, the point of this psychological drama concerns itself with justice in its broadest sense. C.P. Snow has
much to tell us of the human bent of mind, with reference to a
man's effort to right a wrong. Some people prejudge. Some are
swept away by prejudice. Some prefer to be spectators. Some
are afraid to become involved. To all of these reactions, and
many more, described by C.P. Snow, the author declares: "It's
everyone's problem if a man has been wronged."

The Bible would say the same.

U. A TIME FOR RELIGIOUS DRAMA

By this time, we realize that the Bible, although obviously incomplete as far as all aspects of the art form of the theatre, is nevertheless much involved with any play with meaning, since it is the basis for the moral and ethical values of the western world which are the grist of the mill of playwrights. Furthermore, we appreciate the truth that the Biblical spirit can inform a production whether it quotes the Bible or utilizes Biblical situations and heroes or not. Religious drama is frequently where we do not expect it.

"The White House"

Text: Touch not Mine anointed ones,
         And do My prophets no harm.

—Psalms 105:15

Those who attend the straw hat circle theatres this season, will be having reason to doff their chapeaux to Helen Hayes and James Daly appearing in "The White House". This is what happened most recently at the Paper Mill Playhouse where the offering had its first summer showing.

What kind of a play is it? It consists of two acts in which, in the language of the program, "events are depicted . . . relevant and irrelevant, reverent and irreverent . . . in which some of the American presidents and their ladies figure."

Although the play has no single plot, it is somehow more than a series of sketches. "The White House" appears to be more than a piece of scenery or locale of action. It assumes almost a role of its own.

What is significant is that the show has qualities of tragedy, comedy, melodrama and satire contained within itself. What is even more significant, although perhaps less obvious, is that this thoroughly enjoyable theatre piece is a religious drama.

The first act concludes with Abraham Lincoln asking for a Bible on which he swears that his wife, Mary Todd, is not a Confederate spy. The second and final act ends with Helen Hayes reciting a prayer that is hung in the White House. It is a prayer to the effect that those living under the roof of this House shall be good and true.

Both of these final situations in each of the two acts reveal the character of the play. Throughout the performance in its tragic episodes as well as in its humorous ones, there is an unmistakable sense that the White House and those who are part of it have an extra dimension about them.

It is to the credit of the play that it succeeds in conveying in a most enjoyable way the sense of that higher and special quality. As was said before, "The White House" is a religious drama.

V. HOW A CLASSIC IS MADE

The capacity of drama to come alive, to ennoble audiences "to come out of their narrow selves," to feel exalted, is enhanced as it reveals again the Biblical revelation.

"My Fair Lady"

Text: For I give you good doctrine;
         Forsake ye not My teaching.

                                         —Proverbs 4:2

"My Fair Lady" currently showing at the Meadowbrook Dinner Theatre in Milburn is a classic wrapped in a classic. Because it has this double excellence, this musical comedy has become the greatest of its type of all time.

Part of its greatness derives from its theme which is basically the Biblical idea that education is God's great gift to mankind to be utilized for its improvement. Proper education, it should be noted, deals with more than objective pieces of information, such as how to enunciate and pronounce words correctly. It also concerns itself with matters of the heart, such as generous consideration for the feelings of others.

The nature of education was made the core idea of George Bernard Shaw's "Pygmalion" on which "My Fair Lady" is based. The play, with its memorable music and scenery and choreography has become a classic of this genre of theatre in its own first decade of performance.

Thus, in "My Fair Lady", we see a classic musical comedy format presenting a classic Biblical idea with the obvious result—an alltime smash hit.

The play's hero, Professor Higgins, does perform a miracle practically in converting through instruction the ragamuffin Elizah Doolittle into a "lady fair". Elizah, on the other hand, performs a no less, and a far more important miracle, in making the Professor into a humane being.

A full understanding of the miracle of education still escapes us. An appreciation of what makes the play, "My Fair Lady" so truly great is already with us. It is a simple case of a double classic—the best of the Bible presented through the best of Broadway.

VI

Man Distinguished by his Religion

God And His Universe

In a general way, all the preceding chapters have dealt with "religious" subjects, since religion for us means more than just ritual or piety or theology. It means a way of life. In this way of life from the view point of the Bible, we have seen that modern plays and movies have had much interesting material to offer.

For all of this, "religion" has a narrower sense—as well as a wider one. In this narrow sense, religion deals with specific manifestations of God, the meaning of Godhood and the functioning of ecclesiastical institutions and practices in human experience.

Since probably the most decisive differentia of the human being are his "religious concerns", it should not be surprising that serious thinkers and dramatists dealing with man in his various dramatic experiences cannot avoid encountering his religious thoughts, actions and dilemmas.

In this chapter we shall continue to take the path of the Bible from which to examine the collective way of the contemporary theatre in matters theological. In some cases, we shall find the modern road running parallel, and even utilizing the ancient highways and byways. In some instances, there will be a change in direction.

The selections in this chapter are obviously incomplete—as indeed all the chapters have not been intended to be anything like complete treatments of phases of the contemporary theatre. Enough is here, however, to encourage an effort to understand as Hillel Zeitlin, a Yiddish critic, always tried to grasp "how concerned is this poet (in our case, this dramatist) with life and death, with enigmatic existence and absurd death, with man's spirituality, with man's august soul, with the cryptic and conspicuous in nature, with the Creator and his manifestation in mankind's history, etc."

A. SOME ASPECTS OF THE DIVINE

1. God as King

A person may arrive at a concept of God by an examination of his experiences in the world. One of the most common discoveries is the majesty of the universe which leads to a recognition of the Kingship of its Creator.

"Mediterranean Holiday"

Text: And it shall come to pass in the end of days:
That the mountain of the Lord's house shall be
established at the top of the mountains.
—Isaiah 2:2

"Mediterranean Holiday", the latest Cinerama motion picture released by Walter Reade-Sterling is meant to be just what its title says—a pleasant holiday cruise visiting some of the countries which ring the Mediterranean Sea. Norwegian naval cadets aboard The Flying Clipper set sail, at the start of the film, for this trip. It is in their company, as their exploits are filmed, through the excellent medium of Cinerama that this movie's viewers are treated to a real Mediterranean holiday.

If the movie only gave a pictorial view of the sea and various landscapes, along with some fascinating "shots" of interesting social phenomena in each of the nine countries visited, it would be sufficient. A camel fight in Turkey, a spirited dance in Yugoslavia, and an automobile race in Morocco are just some of the thrilling sights afforded.

In addition to all this, however, "Mediterranean Holiday" gives reason to think about man and his religious experiences. Towards the close of the picture, Burl Ives, the commentator, has reference to the pagan civilizations of the Mediterranean community which were recalled in the film. There was for example, a destroyed temple devoted to Baal where human sacrifices had been offered. There was Shum, also, the ancient Egyptian pyramid along with the tomb of Ramses, which had been built by the toil of slave labor.

There can be no mistaking that these ancients had a wrong view of God, and how He should be worshipped. Almost by itself the question arises: "How about us in the modern age? Do we have a more enlightened view of the Eternal, and do we express it more intelligently?"

Although "Mediterranean Holiday", as was mentioned at the outset, is just a most pleasant experience, it may also be the springboard to thinking of the need for achieving the great hoped for time for all mankind. That would be the day when "the mountains of the Lord's house shall be exalted at the top of the mountains, and all nations shall flow unto it . . . Nation shall not lift up sword against nation."

That day would be not only a Mediterranean, but a universal holiday.

2.   God as Father

Almost by itself the idea comes that the majesty of the natural universe bespeaks a need for living in it with a sense of awe, and obedience to a Power greater than one's self. This recognition and submission can come through as a call for kindness as one develops a faith that the universe is friendly. This faith has been expressed in a traditional phrase—the Fatherhood of God. Then, as a natural concommitant of this concept, there has developed the idea of the Brotherhood of Man.

"The Forty-Ninth Cousin"

Text: This is the book of the generations of Adam.
        In the day that God created man,
        in the likeness of God made He him;
        male and female created He them,
        and blessed them, and called their name Adam,
        in the day when they were created.
                                        —Genesis 5:1–5

There are implied in these verses the two main concepts of the Judeo-Christian tradition—the Fatherhood of God and the Brotherhood of Man. That God is Father is expressed in the idea that He is the Creator. That mankind is a brotherhood is conveyed in the thought that all generations are descendants of the common parents—Adam and Eve.

As with all great ideas the basic meaning of these twin religious precepts is so very simple. It is amazing how difficult their application has proven to be in human history. What a better world we would have today if man would accept God as his Father, and every man as his brother!

Because these ideas are so vital for mankind's existence, we should welcome every opportunity that can sensitize us to their significance. Such an opportunity was given recently on the Broadway stage through a play entitled "The Forty-Ninth Cousin".

Menasha Skulnick was the star, but he did not enact the title role. Indeed, he had to be taught the meaning of being a "forty-ninth cousin". He was told by Gerald Hikan, an actor playing the role of a suitor for Skulnick's stage daughter, that "since we are all descended from Adam and Eve, all of us are each other's forty-ninth cousin".

It may have been purely accidental but almost all of the critics in reviewing the play did not explain the meaning of the title. They agreed unanimously that it was a starring vehicle for Skulnick. They said it gave him an excellent medium in which to shine. They did not explain, however, who the forty-ninth cousin is.

Shall we say that they missed the point?

3. The Always Present

Only too well and sadly does our generation know how this faith in the Fatherhood of God and the Brotherhood of Man has been denied. Yet its denial does not mean the non-existence of the ideal. We have all the more to hold on to our faith in it.

"Slow Dance on the Killing Ground"

Text: The earth was desolate and wild . . .
       and the Spirit of God was hovering over the waters.
                                            —Genesis 1:2

"Something blue, something old, something new," is a phrase that applies to bridal attire at the time of a wedding. This same phrase, strangely enough, can be applied to the Broadway play,

"Slow Dance on the Killing Ground", brilliantly written by
William Hanley.

The "blue" in the play is the mood that is shared by each of
the three characters who comprise the entire cast. Mr. Glas is
the Brooklyn candy store owner who lives with a tragic sense
of guilt for having forsaken his wife and child in the days of
Hitler's Germany. Into the store comes Randall, a cape-wearing
Negro who carries an umbrella whose pointed end can be used
to stab a person. Indeed, he has killed his own mother, a pros-
titute. Into the same store, also with a sad lot to bear, comes
Rosie, who has "gotten in trouble". She was looking for an
abortionist. When lost and exhausted, she falls into the store
and lies fainting on the floor.

The "old" in "Slow Dance on the Killing Ground" is a remarkable number of Biblical concepts which are involved.
Ideas such as these are mentioned: love of neighbor, the meaning of heaven and hell, reincarnation, the world as being full
of violence, i.e. "a killing ground". In addition, reference is
made to the need for judgment, and the place of compassion
in the human situation.

What is "new" in the play is a brilliant use of language, as
the very title suggests. Also new is the novel approach or twist
given to the old. Although Randall says of compassion, for
example, that it really has little value, the play develops a keen
and fresh sensitivity to this basic virtue. It is precisely he, who
with Mr. Glas, urges Rosie to save the life of the unborn child!

While "Slow Dance on the Killing Ground" speaks through
one of the characters of life as being a "no man's land", "a
butcher shop", it nevertheless suggests that the dance of life is
to be performed to a music that reveals heart and compassion.
The music is like that of a lark singing over a battlefield. It is
the spirit of God hovering over the deep.

4.   God Is Not an Adolescent

One of the real problems for any generation—and ours faces
it in a most serious form—is to formulate a viable definition
for the three-letter word, "God". So difficult is our situation that
modern theologians have concluded that "God" is dead. Actu-

ally, this startling statement is not so damaging when one realizes how incorrectly the concept of God has been utilized. Sometimes a "lesser" play even more than a major one can reveal truths about our world, and civilization—and as in our case, some crucial element about the modern image of the term "God".

"Love and Kisses"

Text: For my thoughts are not as yours.

—Isaiah 55:8

"Love and kisses" is a simple phrase, familiar to all as a closing line in letters. The other week this phrase appeared on Broadway as the title of a new comedy.

Produced and directed by Dore Schary, starring Larry Parks and Mary Fickett, "Love and Kisses" deals with a marriage of teenagers. The parental home of the groom to which he brings his young bride, is the scene of the play.

The parents are taken by surprise when informed of their son's unexpected marriage. Their trials—especially the father's—and their efforts to keep themselves, and their son and daughter-in-law afloat on the sea of matrimony are the theme of the comedy. Matters are complicated by the fact that their daughter is about to be married, and her marriage is endangered by the developments.

No help can be expected from the young daughter-in-law's parents, for she is fatherless and her mother is an archaeologist, working in Iran (or is it Iraq?). As a wedding gift, the mother sends a mask of an African deity which is worshipped as a home-god. It is a strange god, peculiarly entreated. Whatever the petitioner wants of it must be expressed in an opposite way. Thus, if one desires good health, one prays to it for ill health. If one seeks wealth, one prays to it for poverty.

Taking his cue from his African home-god, the father finds his solution to his problems. He simply tells the young people to do the opposite of what down deep he wishes for them. Thus he succeeds in spreading love and kisses all about.

With all due respect to Bennie (the African deity's name being too complicated to pronounce, it was designated thus simply by the father) the psychology that may work with teen-agers should not be the approach to a divine being. For, in-deed, God's ways are hardly those of teenagers.

5. How to Conceive God?

In the last analysis, it is of tremendous importance to arrive at a belief in moral and spiritual values, a belief in God. Not only personal salvation, but the salvation of mankind as a whole depends upon it. How does one arrive at such a belief? What does such belief—and more precisely, the character of such belief—indicate?

"The Night of the Iguana"

Text: The Lord was not in the wind, nor in the earthquake, nor in the fire, but in the still, small voice.
—I Kings 19:11, 12

A man's conception of God is a reflection of his view of the universe. Since God is the Essence, the Reality of Existence, it follows that what a man thinks of the nature of life is expressed in what he thinks about God. Tell me, then, what a man con-ceives God to be, and I will tell you what that man thinks about the nature of living.

It works the other way, too. Tell me what a man thinks about life, and I will tell you what that man's opinions must be about God.

The Bible gives a beautiful illustration of this in recounting the story of Elijah. The prophet is pictured as fleeing from Jezebel, the wicked queen, whose false prophets he had bested. Alone in a wilderness, hungry and thirsty, he encounters the shattering effects of wind and fire and earthquake. An ordinary mortal would have concluded that God, despite Elijah's loyalty to Him was insensitive to Elijah's needs. So often, indeed, does life appear harsh and cruel, that God may be pictured as being in and of the storm, the fire, and the earthquake of experience.

The true prophet, as Elijah, realizes however, that God is really to be found in the "still, small voice". He is in the good-ness and truth, and beauty of life. It is in the orderliness of the universe, that God appears.

A fascinating treatment of this theme is provided by Tennessee Williams in his play, "The Night of the Iguana", presented recently on Broadway and currently as a movie. The hero of the drama is an "unfrocked" (he claims just to have been "locked out" of the church) minister, T. Laurence Shannon. For him, because his own life bears testimony to such a conception, God is in the lightning. Furthermore, says Shannon, God is a "senile delinquent". No so, says softly, the ninety-seven year old poet and his granddaughter, who figure in the play. For them, there are meaning and beauty and goodness all about them.

This much is sure, dear Reader. When one's life is shaken as by a quake, it is good indeed, to be able to find God gentle, as in a still, small voice.

6. Religious Knowledge—True and False

Since so much is at stake, it is worthwhile to realize how often and how terribly mankind has stumbled and hurt itself in its search for the true and living God.

"Kings of the Sun"

Text: Choose you this day whom ye will serve; whether the Gods which your fathers served that were beyond the River, or the Gods of the Amorites, in whose land ye dwell; but as for me and my house, we will serve the Lord.

—Joshua 24:15

Mankind has had far to go since the first man was created. In trying to understand himself, his neighbors and the universe, man has had much to learn. It is significant that in the realm of science practically every theory that man has developed has proven to be inaccurate. It should not be surprising, therefore, that in the field of philosophy and religion, there should have been held concepts which have been incorrect.

A current motion picture, "Kings of the Sun", starring Yul Brynner, points out how tortuous and difficult has been the path leading to man's knowledge of his relation to the universe and the spirit that informs it. The movie deals with tribes who inhabited northern Mexico much before the white man arrived on the continent. It tells of how they struggled with each other, and of how they understood and misunderstood their responsibilities in the maintenance of their particular religious beliefs. One group believed that the god of fertility and life could be entreated to permit crops to grow if a human sacrifice would be offered. The motion picture shows to an extent the difficulty encountered in ridding the people of this belief.

In this connection one is reminded of the Biblical account of how the children of Israel lived through and with a similar Canaanite practice of human sacrifice to the god Moloch, for example. The Bible records the difficulty in keeping the Hebrews from constantly falling into a similar error.

The movie, "Kings of the Sun", is on reflection more than merely entertaining. It is enlightening as it emphasizes that the Bible is the world's greatest story of mankind's search through the shadows for the meaning of the true God.

B. THE WAYS OF GOD WITH MAN

1. The Spiritual Call

Intuitively, man responds to the call of the wild. Whether by intuition or acculturation, man to be human must respond rather to the call of the spirit.

"But for Whom Charlie"

Text: And the earth was corrupt before God,
and the earth was filled with violence.
                                                —Genesis 6:11

"Injustice is the essence of everything". Thus speaks one of the characters in the new S.N. Behrman play, "But for Whom Charlie", that is now being presented by the Repertory Theatre of Lincoln Center.

To carry out the thought of the essential nature of reality as being immoral and vicious, Behrman states further that so much of human life is characterized by violence. One of the ways in which this characteristic expresses itself is in the fact of "inherited grievances" which so many people feel against their parental backgrounds.

In present-day literature, our playwright points out, frequent themes are bullfights, sadism, and sex. Each of these underscores the tensions and the bitterness which mark contemporary life. In face of this, it is not surprising that the aim of so many people seems to be, as Behrman, puts it "to get even".

The fact is, though, "But For Whom Charlie" would remind us, that there are others who do not agree that moments of truth are achieved through bullfights. They think that "getting even" is indeed proper but only in the sense of returning to society some of the goods inherited from the past. There are people like the fictional Seymour Rosenthal of the play, who in this case, tries through a Foundation to encourage art and artists, truth and those who seek to express it.

On what grounds does Seymour Rosenthal base his actions? What is there in human nature and in human experience to give him reason to pursue his course through his Foundation?

In one of the lines he directs to Faith, a young woman in the play, he says with significant reference to her very name: "Faith, I have very little to offer, but if I had I would offer it to you."

Here then is the upshot of the matter. But for faith, the world would have to be regarded as a jungle. Through faith we may live in it as if it were a temple.

2.   Hard to Maintain Faith

Life seems to be arranged so that man's faith is tested. God leaves it to man to determine and then to hold on to his faith. The ancient Rabbinic dictim expressed it thusly: "Everything is in God's hands; except man's belief in Him".

"One Man's Way"

Text: And God saw everything that He had made, and, behold, it was very good.
—Genesis 1:31

Only be strong, and of good courage.
—Joshua 1:18

"One Man's Way" is a current moving picture based on the biography of the famous minister, Norman Vincent Peale.

It begins with a scene in Dr. Peale's father's church where

the elder Peale, a minister himself, is interrupted at services by his son, Norman. The youngster had felt constrained to object forcefully to some other boy who had called him a sissy because he was a minister's son. It soon becomes clear that Norman is unhappy with being a minister's child, and is opposed to any suggestion that he might grow up to be a minister.

As he develops, however, he turns to the ministry. The picture shows him as a student at the Theological School of Boston University. Upon graduation, he is placed in a small church in Rhode Island. After a period of service, he goes from there to a church in Syracuse. While in this university town, he meets a coed whom he courts determinedly. At first she demurred because she believed that the ministry could not provide what she wanted—a life of excitement and independence.

Having been highly successful in Syracuse, he accepts a call to a distinguished church in New York City. Here he develops into the nationally famous, "the best known preacher" in America.

Through all of this he becomes associated with his special message labeled "the power of positive thinking". Simply put—simplification is inadequate for complete interpretation, of course—his thesis is that God made the world and man as "good". Whatever is wrong with a man's life can be set right by a man utilizing God's resources within him and about him. The point is that a man believing in God may courageously meet life with every prospect for success.

Interestingly and strangely, Dr. Peale's biographical film reveals the times where he himself faltered in his own positive thinking. The point is that it is not easy to hold on to one's faith. Furthermore, the movie reports the controversy which has raged about Peale's doctrine by his fellow theologians. All in all, "One Man's Way" although highly to be recommended, may have to be re-routed somewhat before it can become the Way for all to go.

3.   The Universality and Contemporaneity of the Call

What is discouraging—and here is where faith must function additionally—is the fact that mankind seems to be making little progress in becoming more truly civilized.

"Lawrence of Arabia"

Text: Now the priest of Midian had seven daughters;
        and they came and drew water and filled the troughs
        to water their father's flock.
        And the shepherds came and drove them away;
        but Moses stood up and helped them, and watered
        their flock.

                                        —Ecclesiastes 2:16, 17

The Bible reflects the important role that a well of water played in the life of the people of Biblical lands and times. Understandably, a well, and particularly, an oasis, was associated with life-giving qualities, both physical and spiritual. Interestingly, this same pool of water could elicit the most savage reactions. Man would pillage and plunder, and kill if need be, to take possession of fountains of water.

Moses is reported to have protected the daughters of his future father-in-law in one case where they were threatened by brigands who sought to deprive the girls of their possession of a well.

This Biblical incident may come to mind in viewing the award-winning film, "Lawrence of Arabia". The moving picture has one scene in which an Arab shoots in cold blood a fellow-Arab for daring to draw water from the first Arab's well.

Noting the savagery of this action, Lawrence, a newcomer to the desert, is pictured in the film as being appalled.

As the story unfolds, and Lawrence becomes more and more like an Arab, he is shown to lose his "civilized" standards. This transformation takes place with quite some soul-searching, it is true.

At the same time it is shown that the motives of the so-called "civilized" nations, England and France, are not so noble either. Lawrence, who has been sent by England to insure the Arabs' participation in the First World War against Turkey recognized the chicanery of British diplomacy as not different from the trickiness of the Arab chieftains.

What happened cruelly about a pool of water centuries ago, is continued in modern times with greater ferocity, especially about pools of oil. "Lawrence of Arabia" teaches that the call of the wild needs yet to be silenced by the call of the spirit.

4. Modern Science Means Reinterpretation

To confound confusion, it seems, the very fact that modern science has helped explain many of life's mysteries, has put the faith in God as He was apprehended before the advent of modern knowledge under new strain. It seems as if God requires constant searching after Him.

"Gideon"

Text: The story of Gideon.

—Judges 6–8

The Biblical Book of Judges concerns itself with those individual champions of the Israelites who arise from time to time during the centuries of Israel's settlement in Canaan following the exodus from Egypt. It was the function of these "judges" as they were called, to lead the Israelites in defense of their freedom against neighboring oppressors. One such hero was Gideon.

The Bible tells of his personal exploits and of the divine miracles that were performed in his career. Paddy Chayefsky, after much scholarly research, has written a play about Gideon. One of the fascinating facets of this latest play by Chayefsky is that he makes God an active participant on the stage as He converses with Gideon. The role of God has been performed by Frederick March. Gideon's part was portrayed by Douglas Campbell. Both acted brilliantly.

Equally challenging as his endeavor to present God on stage, was Chayefsky's treatment of the basic theme of the play. The argument advanced by Gideon and some of his friends is that man's salvation is in man's hands alone. The miracles that happened were not divine manifestations. They were naturalistic or socio-economic facts that could be explained humanistically or scientifically. Indeed, God Himself, is given these words to say at the close of the play:

"God no more believes it odd
That man can not believe in God".

This is an interesting switch for Chayefsky. In his "Tenth

Man" he had quite a different conclusion. There he had the young man come to recognize the power of the spirit in the modern world.

I suppose we can say that in "Gideon", Chayefsky was bringing mentality of New York to Jerusalem. In the "Tenth Man" he was bringing the spirit of Jerusalem to New York.

The road is more felicitous the latter way.

5. Man Proposes, God Disposes

When faith in God is hard put to defend itself, there is always the amazing and impressive fact that in a way which seems to be far more than accidental, life frequently takes a most unexpected turn, and faith is restored.

"Any Number Can Win"

Text: And Absalom was riding upon the mule,
        and the mule went under the thick boughs of a great
            terebinth,
        and his head caught hold of the terebinth,
        and he was taken up between the heaven and the
            earth . . .

—II Samuel 18:9

While telling a gripping story, "Any Number Can Win", a motion picture featuring Jean Gabin, makes a far-reaching observation about life.

The film recounts a superbly planned effort to rob a gambling casino. A photograph, unexpectedly taken, proves to be the plotter's undoing.

Here then, is the situation—a most carefully thought through design for action is brought to nought by a minor circumstance that could hardly have been expected.

This situation gives rise to the idea that so much of life reveals this same kind of frustration. Some insignificant, unexpected matter can wreck a most elaborate human scheme, meant for either good or ill. Robert Burns expressed this theme poetically, "The best laid schemes of mice and men gang aft agley".

The popular proverb expresses it so: "Man proposes, God disposes."

Whether the "best laid plans" are shattered through accident
or Providence, it is not our intention to discuss here. Suffice it
to say that the Bible recognized this characteristic of the human
experience.

Absalom, a most handsome son of King David, is reported in
the Bible to have rebelled unsuccessfully against his father. In
fleeing from the victorious royal forces, he is captured and killed
when his long hair was caught by some low-lying branches of a
tree.

Yes, life seems to be a game of chance in which any number
can win. Similarly, any number can lose. Frequently, strangely,
the crucial number is one which was not expected to figure at
all!

For Absalom, it was his hair. For Jean Gabin in the movie it
was a photograph. For each of us, who knows what it is?

6.   God's Ways In History

a.   A Mystery

No matter how much study is devoted to the meaning of God
in human experience, always there is a point of arrival at mystery. God's ways, in the last analysis, are past man's finding out
not only in any individual's life, but in that of society as a
whole.

"A Man for All Seasons"

Text: The Books of Chronicles.

The Books of Chronicles I and II are Biblical history. This
is a special kind of history. It is history with divine involvement.

The Books of Chronicles tell of the generations of Adam until the decree of Cyrus (536 B.C.E.) which permitted the Jewish
exiles in Babylonia to return to their homes in Palestine. In
these Chronicles the royal houses of the Jewish people figure
prominently. Unmistakably, the point is made that those in
power were expected to recognize their relationship to God's
laws of righteousness and religion. A proper respect for the

divine way brings blessing. A disregard of God's rules by Israel's monarchs means disaster—personal and national.

Although the kings are thus seen to be central in the development of events for the people as a whole, the Bible nevertheless suggests that the prophetic urge for righteousness is in the heart of each individual. Therefore, the Bible teaches, you must have good people, not only good kings, to have good laws kept properly. Then you may expect prosperity and victory.

The matter does not work out so simply, however. God, wonderously, determines what happens. It is He who finally controls the events of history, although in some mysterious way, the common man and royalty have something to do with the unfolding of destiny.

Now at the City Center, the famous play, "A Man for all Seasons", deals with Sir Thomas More's life and death as these were affected by royalty and the common man in medieval England. Most significant is More's determination to maintain his conviction that God's laws supercede a mortal king's desires. For this noble principle, he forfeits his life while the common man remains disinterested.

Since More was right and the king and common man were wrong, the play raises the mystifying question, "Where was God's Hand in all of this?"

Because of this question, dear Reader, "A Man for all Seasons" may well be considered a mystery play—although not billed as such.

b. A Fulfillment of a Promise

One of the strangest—if not the most unbelievable—stories of mankind is the survival of the Jewish people. To add to this mystery wrapped in a riddle is the truth that the people had remained creative through the four millennia of its existence. Could it be the carrying out of an ancient divine compact concerning the land and people of Israel?

"Exodus"

Text: The Book of Exodus.

Exodus, the second of the Five Books of Moses, derives its name from its contents. It tells of the experiences of the children of Israel before, during and for forty years after their leaving Egypt where they had lived for several hundred years.

It is in this Biblical book that we find the Ten Commandments, as well as many of the other precepts and laws which became the basic constitution and bylaws of the Jewish people, and ultimately, for a good part of western civilization.

Significant is the fact that many of these statutes have reference to the land of Israel. Whatever interpretation may be given for this, the fact of the association of the land with a full expression of the Hebrew civilization underscores the truth that the Jewish genius expressed itself most creatively when the Land of Promise was somehow involved.

In this connection, the recent film "Exodus," has produced an interesting result. Based on Leon Uris' book by that name, the motion picture has left its mark chiefly by reason of its musical theme.

Part of this theme had been composed before the picture. Part of it was written for this film. It was only in the combination needed as a theme for "Exodus", that the music by composer Gold achieved its fulfillment.

Here again, it seems as if the ancient Biblical truth has come to light in our times. From out of Zion, comes a birth of creativity for the world's improvement and delight.

Indeed, actual physical living in the land of Israel is not necessary. It is sufficient that the land be a direction.

After all, the Decalogue was promulgated in the wilderness while the children of Israel were on the way to the Holy Land.

7. Reward and Punishment

a. Let There Be Order

One of the most basic concepts of Biblical theology is that the Creator of the universe is also the Master of the universe, the Judge and Law-giver of mankind. The following selections from current plays and movies indicate how modern, yet ancient—and how naturally accepted in our theatre—are the considerations of God's ways with man.

"Richard III"

Text: In the beginning God created the heavens and the
       earth.
       And the earth was void and empty, and darkness was
          on the face of the deep;
       and the spirit of God moved over the waters.
       And God said: "Let there be light." And there was
          light.

                                              —Genesis 1:1–3

This year's quadricentennial of the birth of William Shakespeare has stimulated many productions of his plays. A number
of his works have been appearing as motion pictures. In some
cases these are reissues especially because of the current com-
memoration. Among the latter, one should mention for special
distinction the Lawrence Olivier starring production of "Richard III". The same play has received excellent reviews for its
splendid presentation at the Stratford, Connecticut Shakespeare
Festival.

Known as one of Shakespeare's historical plays, "Richard
III" tells of the Machiavellian efforts of the one who plays the
central role, and gives the title to the play, to wrest the English
crown for himself. Coming at the close of the War of the Roses,
the events described in this Shakespearian play are replete with
murder, chicanery and chaos. The chaotic conditions prevailing
in England at that time called for someone to put the affairs of
state in order.

Richard III took advantage of the situation. The type of
order he instituted, however, led only to more chaos.

Fortunately, as Shakespeare informs us, albeit indirectly, the
nature of the universe in general, and the world of man particularly, is such that, as the Bible teaches, there is a Providence
which is a spirit hovering over the waters. This is the spirit that
brings light where there is darkness, and order out of chaos.

At this Quadricentennial, let us render unto Shakespeare the
things that are Shakespeare's—his genius as a playwright and
poet. Let us rediscover too, that the fundamental truths he
teaches—such as those in "Richard III"—are the things of the
Bible.

b. Reward Reserved for the Righteous

A cardinal principle of faith in God's conduct of the world is that the righteous are blessed for their righteousness.

"The Best Man"

Text: And thou shalt love thy neighbor as thyself.
—Leviticus 19:18

The Republican and the Democratic parties are readying themselves for their National Conventions and the voice of the politicians is heard ever louder in the land. At the actual conventions, the voice with many different accents and emphases will announce, "We want to nominate a man who. . ." and then will proceed to list the qualifications of the proposed candidates for the highest office in America.

These would-be nominees—avowed and non-avowed—will have used stratagems and means by the time of the national political assemblies, as indeed they will continue to do through the proceedings, to effect their nomination. It is at these sessions that the hope is piously expressed even by the antagonists to each other: "May the best man win".

It is this "best man" who is the subject and gives the title to Gore Vidal's recent Broadway success, now being issued as a moving picture. In his work, Mr. Vidal presents much of the heart of America as it beats louder and faster at its national selection of standard bearers for each of the major political parties.

Mr. Vidal reveals much of the "dirty politics" that is played, but he also shows that basically the American system is geared to a true belief in God—not a mere taking of His name in vain. Additionally, the real leader America accepts, Mr. Vidal insists, must be "sensitive to other people".

A man who recognizes the God-given, equal rights to life, liberty, and the pursuit of happiness of all Americans, rights guaranteed by the Constitution, is a good American. He is equally a good man who lives according to the Biblical injunction of love of neighbor. He is the one who can expect reasonably to be accepted by Americans as the best man, for there is no "best" except as it is first based on "good".

c. Retribution is Sure for the Sinner

A concomitant of the idea that the righteous prosper is that the wicked fail and suffer.

"The World of Henry Orient"

Text: He that planted the ear, shall He not hear?
He that formed the eye, shall He not see? . . .
The Lord knoweth the thoughts of many,
That they are vanity.

—Psalms 94:9, 11

"The World of Henry Orient" is more than a funny film featuring Peter Sellers. It has a most important lesson of the spirit to impart which it does interestingly, indeed.

The very title of the picture is meant to tell something of the meaning of its story. The Orient is associated in the western man's mind with mystery, adventure and secret escapades. The hero's name, Henry Orient, suggests that his "world" is one of intrigue.

Into his life, as the picture tells it, two teenage girls enter. These two follow him about because one of them has made him her ideal and her idol. In the course of their adventurous juvenile pursuit of him, they discover that this idol of theirs hardly deserves their adoration.

As Henry Orient recognizes that he is being observed by these children, he assumes that they were intent on spying on him. In this uneasiness about being discovered in his philanderings, lies part of his punishment.

This is the way of divine retribution, it seems. There are always eyes that see and ears that hear a person's backsliding. There are no secret, hidden things even in what a man may consider his private "orient".

For a teenager's escapades, this discovery is not crushing, because a youngster's secret world is in most cases just juvenile adventuring. With the coming of adulthood, troubles become more real, and indiscretions more and more serious.

It is in a grown-up's "orient" that the truly sinister lurks, only inevitably to be brought to light. It is through this being brought into the light, that the semi-darkness of devious designs disappears, and the designer meets his undoing.

d. The Way of Atonement

To redeem the sinner, to save him from a punishment that might crush him, there is the way of atonement open to him.

"The Small World of Sammy Lee"

Text: Righteousness guardeth him that is upright
         in the way;
         But wickedness overthroweth the sinner.

—Proverbs 13:6

There is a familiar axiom which claims that nothing succeeds like success, and nothing fails like failure. The truth of this proposition is bourne in upon us from any sides. Let a man be known to be successful, then many opportunities are presented to him to continue his success. Let him, however, be known to have failed, then less opportunities for success are afforded him, and the chances for continued failure are thereby increased.

Proverbs among the people today express this truth variously. Thus we may hear it said: Money goes to money. On the other hand we know: One lie leads to another. As in business, so in ethics, one success leads to a second, and one error begets another.

It is in this sense that the Biblical Book of "Proverbs" states that "righteousness guards the righteous, and wickedness continues to conquer the wicked". How then, can a sinner break this vicious chain that binds him constantly?

Allusion to this question is made in the splendid film, "The Small World of Sammy Lee", featuring Anthony Newley. Playing the role of Sammy Lee, a small town actor, Mr. Newley brilliantly conveys what happens to the actor who because of gambling debts becomes more and more involved with a racketeering loan shark and with shady operations to repay the loan. His small world becomes smaller, practically crushing the life out of him.

It is only after he receives his punishment literally at the hands of the racketeer's henchmen—Sammy Lee is severely beaten—that the way seems to be cleared finally for him to break free from the chain of transgression that compresses his ever-diminishing world. Sadly but truly, there is no atonement without pain, neither in Sammy Lee's world, nor in ours.

e. Poetic Justice

The Biblical tradition seems to have regarded poetic justice as being the finest expression of divine justice. That tradition has its appeal today.

"Vertigo"

Text: And Pharaoh charged all his people, saying:
"Every son that is born ye shall cast into the river . . ."
—Exodus 1:22
And the waters returned, and covered the chariots and the horsemen, even all the host of Pharaoh.
—ibid. 14:28

An Alfred Hitchcock murder mystery bears the stamp of the master. Whether his tales are recounted on television or in the movies, there is something special about a Hitchcock thriller. The story is somewhat stranger. The acting is sharper. The direction is keener. All in all, if other mysteries are prosaic, a Hitchcock production, as a work of art, is a piece of poetry.

Come to think of it, what lends special poignancy to a Hitchcock opus is that usually the justice that is meted out partakes of the character of poetry. It is poetic justice.

Where a case of poetic justice is presented, there you find a kind of surprising rhyme and reason between the crime, the criminal and his or her comeuppance. A fine example of this is contained in the Hitchcock motion picture "Vertigo", starring James Stewart and Kim Novak.

The fundamental point of the story is made when unexpectedly the criminal dies by the very same instrumentality that was used to kill the innocent victim.

Such poetic justice has a hold on the human spirit because it seems to reflect that there must be an orderer of events if they work out in such an orderly fashion. Can rhyme, reason and poetry be accidental? Do these not imply an overall systematizer?

The Biblical tradition has reference to such a universal state of affairs in the instance of Pharaoh's involvement with the children of Israel. Through water, he sought to destroy them when he decreed that all their male babies should be cast into the River Nile. Through water, he is punished when he and his troops are drowned in the Red Sea.

When such poetic justice occurs in a Hitchcock story, you have a master's thriller-diller. When it takes place in real life, you may see the hand of the Master of the universe.

f. The Box

The Biblical authors knew that life only too frequently failed to reveal the functioning of God's justice. The question was raised in Scriptures: "Why do the righteous suffer and the wicked prosper?" That question—with the attempt at its answer —is appropriate not only in the Bible, but on Broadway today since it still springs so often from the human spirit.

"Golden Boy"

Text: Wilt Thou harass a driven leaf, and wilt Thou pursue
the dry stubble?

—Job 13:25

Then Job answered the Lord and said: "Behold, I
am of small account; what shall I answer Thee?
I lay my hand upon my mouth."

—ibid 40:3, 4

In a recent article (N.Y. Times, Sunday, October 18, 1964), William Gibson, who was called in to doctor the script of Clifford Odets' "Golden Boy" for its Broadway musical version, had something interesting to say about finding the deeper meaning of this new production.

In the original drama, the hero Joe Bonaparte, was torn between becoming a violinist or getting rich quick as a boxer. In the new version, the central figure, renamed Joe Wellington, is a Negro who suffered from several conflicts. First, he has to choose between his father's wish that he abstain from fighting and his own desire to raise himself out of Harlem by his fists. Then he must resolve the conflict of his love for a white girl, which is really part of the larger problem of whether to move into white society or remain with his own race.

Writes Gibson in this regard: "This is an individual story between a Negro and a white girl. But if people want to read larger meanings into it they are welcome".

Accepting Mr. Gibson's invitation to interpret more broadly the allegory of the Golden Boy, we might note the fact that in both versions of the play the hero is a boxer. In both cases he is striving to fight back against a sea of troubles, hopefully, as Shakespeare put it, "by opposing to end them".

All of his struggles, as indeed his very life, are symbolized in this occupation of "boxer". The root of the word "box" implies something constraining, restraining, imprisoning. The boxer is not only the fighter who wants to break free, but also the contestant who is boxed in.

In the play there are quite a few verbal references, as well as stage props and settings to point up this boxed-in situation in which many people find themselves. The office where she works, says the heroine is for her like a jail. His black skin, for Joe, is a prison from which he can not escape. Indeed, one character says directly to Joe: "They've got you in a box".

This sense of being boxed was experienced by Job in the Bible, who cried out that God had hedged him in (Job 3:20). The Biblical Job, like Golden Boy, lashed out—to his own hurt.

The Golden Boy finally committed suicide. Job learned, however, that there are times in life when one can only roll with the punch. Fortunate is he who knows when and how.

C. THE WAYS OF MAN WITH GOD

1. Free to Choose

To the concept of "reward and punishment", there must be a pre-condition, namely—"man's freedom of will". Unless a man can choose to be either righteous or villainous, there is no reason to reward or punish him.

As has been seen so often in our reviews, a play unlikely to be considered a source for theological insights may be a carrier of some fundamental religious truth.

"Poor Richard"

Text: Behold I have set before you life and death—
        and you shall choose life.

                                      —Deuteronomy 30:19

Jean Kerr surely must have discovered that the soul of wit is more than just brevity. It is rather a wisdom which surpasses ordinary human understanding, requiring, in fact, a rare native intelligence.

Already famous for her "Mary, Mary", not to mention other works, the authoress is now represented by "Poor Richard" on Broadway. Again there shines forth the soul of her wit which is a penetrating wisdom about human nature and the human condition.

Her "poor" Richard is a poet who is being lionized. He himself, for all his bravado, has a sneaking, poor opinion of himself. To help him achieve a more correct ability to live with himself —necessary before he can live properly with others—he has the love of a young secretary. In the course of the play, one of the most meaningful comments made is: "Worse than having no hope, is having no alternatives."

This is a truly wise saying which points up the great merit of Biblical religion.

The Bible teaches that man has had a divine gift bestowed upon him in that he has been given free will. Man can choose his way to live. He may be good or evil. The choices and the alternatives are his.

The Bible, of course, urges that man shall choose the good for this is the alternative that means life.

Frequently, a person makes a wrong choice of the path in life to follow. In this he will suffer and perhaps curse his lot.

It is then that the Bible would remind him that although the choice was wrong, the exercise of freedom of will is nevertheless a great privilege. This is not only true for Jean Kerr's "poor" Richard, but for every Tom, Dick and Harry.

2. Let Us Pray

Along with man's freedom of will, the Biblical tradition teaches that there are also God's omnipotence and omniscience.

How these can operate together, especially with the further theological dogma of predestination is a profound mystery. How can man choose his way of life when God knows beforehand what he will do, and can force him to do His divine will?

What is clear, nevertheless, is that man finds himself often—in fact, at the most crucial moments of his life—in need of some power greater than himself.

"Fail Safe"

Text: And He said: "Lay not thy hand upon the lad . . .
        for now I know that thou art a God-fearing man . . ."
                                              —Genesis 22:12

The President of the United States is talking with his former school chum who is now a General in the Air Force. The Commander-in-Chief is requesting his dear, trusted friend to do something most unusual. He is asking that two atomic bombs be dropped on an unsuspecting, defenseless New York City. This command is being issued, oddly enough, because the President sees it as his patriotic duty to have this done.

How this strange and ghastly situation has come to pass, is explained by the motion picture, "Fail Safe" (based on the well known work of fiction by the same name). Suffice it to say that a mechanical failure has triggered a series of events which finally brings the American President to the need for such a directive to destroy New York City in order to save the rest of the world from atomic annihilation.

In making his request of the aviator, the President reminds his friend of their school days when in chapel they listened to sermons dealing with Abraham's willingness to sacrifice his beloved son, Isaac, to prove his faithfulness to God. This citation of Biblical writ is made to point up the need of both the President and the General to destroy their own beloved in order to prove their faithfulness to Russia whose Moscow has been bombed through error.

All in all, there is no mistaking the fact that "Fail Safe" has a sermonic message. It seeks to alert the world to the horrors that lie in wait for it both through design and mischance. It is a sermon that naturally leads to prayer.

"As Abraham, so may we hear God's voice delivering us and
our dear ones from the need of the most dreadful of sacrifices—
the slaughter of our children by ourselves."

3. The Never Failing

Prayer is as natural to man as breathing. There is no human
life which does not find itself at times dependent upon a source
of never-failing encouragement. Man has religious needs which
he may deny, but which he ultimately must satisfy.

"Ben Franklin in Paris"

Text: A merry heart maketh a cheerful countenance;
        But by sorrow of heart the spirit is broken.

                                                —Proverbs 15:13

Just how much of historical fact is in the story of the current
musical hit "Ben Franklin in Paris" may be left to students of
history. How close to the real personality is the stage presentation of Benjamin Franklin may be a proper matter for his bi-
ographers. The fact that there are history and biography in this
charming production is enough to make it not only a most entertaining, but also an unusually meaningful musical.

The action centers around the efforts of the one-time Phila-
delphia printer to win recognition from the King of France of
the independent statehood of the thirteen colonies revolting
against England. This recognition was crucial for the success
of the newly declared United States of America. It meant,
among other things, sorely needed arms and ammunition for
the Revolutionary Army.

Even as it was crucial, so was it a difficult assignment. It required all the political skill and mental adroitness of a gifted
man such as Benjamin Franklin. In portraying his efforts to
achieve his goal, the brilliant Robert Preston as "Ben Franklin
in Paris" gives flashes of insight into the personality of America's
first ambassador to France.

By his own admission, Franklin was an agnostic. He taught,
nevertheless, the need for facing life's tasks with positive opti-

mism, which fundamentally means a certain measure of faith. The musical has a charming number on the point declaring that a smile is half the battle. The Biblical Book of Proverbs—an older and much more authentic version of wisdom than Poor Richard's Almanac— affirms that a cheerful countenance, so necessary to win the battle, has to come from the heart. Poor Ben, the agnostic, may have thought of that when he did not find it in his heart to smile. It was then he must have taken to his knees.

4. Priest and/or Prophet and True Religion

Genuine religion is the great hope of the world. A false or even watered-down version of religion can be most damaging for the redemption and salvation—physical as well as spiritual—of mankind.

Without denying the need and value for the priestly functions of true religion, the Bible has also emphasized its prophetic responsibilities. The following three examples from our current theatre show aspects of Scriptural principles—(1) the fact that the priesthood and the prophetic callings are not mutually exclusive, (2) that every true believer in God is expected to serve as one of His prophets in a certain sense, and (3) the great courage needed for the prophetic enterprise can come only from the sincere faith that prompts it in the first place.

a. *"The Cardinal"*

Text: And the word of the Lord came unto me saying . . .
        I have appointed thee a prophet unto the nations . . .
        Say not I am a child. For to whomsoever I shall send
        thee thou shalt go . . . Be not afraid of them."
                                        —Jeremiah 1:4-8

The motion picture, "The Cardinal" is not just a Catholic, or even only a Christian film; it is a movie which deals with religion. Anyone devoted to the meaning of true religion can find much in the picture to occupy his attention and win his approval.

The story of the movie revolves around a priest who rises to the high rank of Cardinal in the Roman Catholic Church. His rise covers years of his life during which he experiences the deepest and the highest of human emotions. He is brought face to face with life at its noblest and its most beautiful as well as at its most degrading and most disgusting. Through all of this, his religious persuasion is with him to guide and inspire. Even where he is on temporary leave from his official priestly function, this religious influence does not forsake him.

A viewer of the film may note the fact as gradually appreciated by the priest, himself, that maturity brings with it a finer interpretation of the priestly calling. One may be impressed too, with the truth that the priest has a major service to perform, not only as a priest, but as a prophet.

The film pictures the fact that true religion has a relevance to life, especially in its most critical aspects. Without downgrading the value of liturgy, "The Cardinal" may be understood to regard the verse of Jeremiah as the proper motto for a religious leader. "Behold I have set thee as a Prophet to the Nations. Whatsoever I shall command thee, thou shalt speak."

Adherence to this principle renders a prince of the Church, a prince of a man. It can do the same for every truly religious person.

b. *"The Deputy"*

Text: Ye are My witnesses.

—Isaiah 43:10

Now that "The Deputy", the controversial play by Rolf Hochhuth, has been showing on the New York stage for some time, we are in a position to assess some of the fears and the hopes which accompanied its opening.

There was the fear that it might lead to rioting, as was the case in some of the play's presentations in several European cities. There was the further apprehension that the cause of goodwill in inter-faith relations would suffer irreparable harm. Additionally, there was the uncertainty whether American democracy, guaranteeing freedom of expression, would prove equal to the pressures being placed upon it.

Along with these possible embarrassments, there were certain hopes which were entertained by those who would present the play to American audiences. It was hoped that a true, historical account of one phase of those dark days of Hitlerian persecution would help explain and make clear the grievous condition into which segments of mankind had sunk—as persecutor, persecuted and onlooker. Understanding the fact of the Pope's not declaring publicly his abhorrence, specifically of the destruction of the millions of defenceless Jews by the Nazis, while helping the victims secretly, it was hoped would have a salutory effect on the future.

What has happened with these fears and hopes? Not all of them have materialized, nor have all of them been in vain, or unfounded.

One result is certain, though. An acquaintance with the play —by reading it, or better by actually viewing it—must result in sensitizing one to the moral requirement of opposing evil and injustice wherever these lift their ugly heads.

The Judeo-Christian tradition of the Bible declares that all decent human beings, all who may aspire to be His people, are expected to be witnesses for God.

Although not every one may be the Deputy, everyone is expected to be a deputy to represent God. Especially is such representation necessary when it is most difficult. This is the sad and tragic case, whenever the world or any part of it, appears to be God-forsaken.

c. "Luther"

Text: And Abraham stretched forth his hand, and took the
        knife to slay his son . . . And the angel of the
        Lord said: "Lay not thy hand upon the lad . . . "
                                        —Genesis 22:10, 12
        But the righteous shall live by his faith.
                                        —Habakkuk 2:4

The playwright, John Osborne, is considered correctly to be one of the group of "angry young men" who have made such a stir in and out of England. One of his famous plays is entitled appropriately enough, "Look Back in Anger".

It is not surprising that a most fitting hero for a play by him would be naturally enough an angry young man, Luther. It was Luther who as we all know, sparked the revolt of Protestantism against the Roman Catholic Church of his day.

Osborne's "Luther" is presently being enacted on Broadway. In the course of the play, the lead character finds reason to explain that life, especially for one who would be honestly critical, is instinct with death, even as death is strangely implanted with life. To prove his point, the stage Luther cites the story of Abraham's near sacrifice of his beloved son, Isaac.

Luther in his protestations has certainly affected the history of the world as well as the development of the Christian Church. Moreover, he has given a dramatic example of the fact that living dangerously must be accepted as the way of life for anyone who seeks the truth.

A good question is: where or how does one find the courage to live thus precariously? Osborne, through his character Luther, quotes without mentioning by name, the prophet Habakkuk who said: "The righteous shall live by his faith".

One of the most moving scenes in the play on Broadway takes place when Luther challenges a colleague: "You say, 'I believe in the forgiveness of sins!' Do you?" In other words, the basic question is, how deep and real is the faith professed? This is the crucial question, not only on Broadway but wherever Biblical living is taken seriously.

5. In While Out of This World

Even mysteries are not exempt because they deal with matters "out of this world" from the moral and ethical consequences in this world according to true religion.

"The Tenth Man"

Text: The Book of Ezekiel.

Of all the prophetical books of the Bible, that of Ezekiel is the most esoteric. It contains the mystical vision that the prophet had of heaven. "Thus did the cherubim lift up their wings, and the wheels were beside them; and the glory of the

God of Israel was over them above". (Ch. 11, v. 22) This and other verses like it made Ezekiel the father of the later mysticism of the Judeo-Christian tradition. Through all of this Ezekiel has remained mysterious and his vision beyond ordinary comprehension.

Yet it is to him that we should direct our attention if we are to understand the action that takes place in Paddy Chayefsky's recent Broadway play, "The Tenth Man". The plot revolves around a Dybbuk. Very few people know what is meant by a Dybbuk, which is a Hebrew word. Fewer still know Ezekiel's relation to it.

By "Dybbuk" is meant the soul of a dead person who because of having sinned while alive cannot achieve salvation. In this unsaved state the soul may then enter into the body of some living person. When this occurs, great spiritual disturbance results for the "possessed".

Only by exorcising the Dybbuk can peace come. The knowledge of how to perform this exorcism has been reserved among certain spiritualists called Kabbalists. This wisdom originally derived from a study of Ezekiel's mysticism.

Paddy Chayefsky makes the account of a modern exorcism the business of his play. It is a fascinating and dramatic presentation.

Another fact should be borne in mind by the play viewer. Although the concept of a Dybbuk has been familiar among Jewish mystics, it did not function as a vital factor in normative Judaism. Similarly, Ezekiel is remembered not so much for his vision of Heaven, as his directives for human life here on Earth.

6. Needed: A New Spirit

Sensitive dramatists concerned with man in his individual, social and national life, and with special problems of our generation must recognize the need for a rebirth of the spirit of genuine religion.

"The West Side Story"

Text: Cast away from you all your transgressions
wherein ye have transgressed;

and make you a new heart and a new spirit;
for why will ye die, O house of Israel?"
—Ezekiel 18:31

The winning of many awards both as a play and as a moving picture signalizes Leonard Bernstein's "The West Side Story" as an unusual contribution to the American cultural treasury.

Reminiscent of Shakespeare's Romeo and Juliet, "The West Side Story" tells of a beautiful love of a young man and a young woman which ends in tragedy. Because they have different backgrounds, their love is frowned upon by their respective groups. One of the groups—the girl's people—is Puerto Rican which as the newcomer to the West Side of New York City is engaged in gang warfare with the already established whites in the neighborhood. The young man being of the latter group, is finally destroyed by misguided hatred and distrust of the girl's people. Whereupon, her life is brought to nought also.

The destruction of young lives with their love is so senseless and unnecessary that it makes us wonder, "Why and how long must this go on?" It reminds us of Ezekiel's call to the children of Israel which may be paraphrased to read: "Cast away your transgressions. Do away with your foolish cruelties and zeal for vengeance. Get a new spirit into your hearts—the spirit of understanding and good will. Why do you insist upon destroying beauty and goodness and life itself?"

This burning question, ringed with pain and sorrow, arises not only out of a story from New York City's West Side. It is a query natural to our modern world situation. May the answer of human intelligence and good will soon be heard throughout the land. Then shall the East Side and West Side be at peace, and the Iron Curtain be no more.

7. Faith's Victims

Like everything good, faith can be abused. Needing it, finding life unbearable without it, men and women are so anxious for belief that they can be easily duped by unconscionable people who take advantage of them.

a. The Dirty Trick

"Bajour"

Text: When thou art come into the land that the Lord
giveth thee . . . there shall not be found among you
. . . one that doeth divination, a soothsayer or a sor-
cerer . . .

—Deuteronomy 18:9, 10

Gypsies have a language of their own. It is a language that
they can speak but not write. This is because the language has
no alphabet.

A word of this Gypsy tongue is becoming familiar to theatre-
goers these days. The word, "Bajour", which means "swindle"
is the title of a rousing musical comedy currently showing on
Broadway.

The play tells of a widow who loses part of her deceased husband's insurance money to a Gypsy band. The lady had been
convinced by one of the tribe that this money bore a curse
which had to be removed. As it works out, the money itself is
separated from her through a Bajour, a good old Gypsy swindle.

How come that the Gypsies ply their Bajour tricks success-
fully and so often? An answer is provided by one of the characters in the play who suggested that those who are duped find
themselves in need of something which the Gypsies seem to
offer. These are lonely folks in search of a faith for their future.
Hence they turn to Gypsies who read palms, tea leaves, cards,
etc. and furnish them what they need. In the process, they are
duped and swindled.

The sad fact is that there is a strong and cruel tendency on
the part of some people to take advantage of their fellows, especially when the latter are in desperate need. "Playing on the
emotions" is a well known way in which taking of advantage is
being practiced. It is precisely when someone's heart is broken
and the eyes filled with tears that one can become prey to un-
scrupulous charlatans.

The Bible recognized this state of affairs. It knew that the
need of human beings for faith is as strong and urgent as the

need for food. Scriptures understood that sometimes for survival
and happiness, faith is even more necessary than bread.

To lead astray unfortunate people when they are desperately
seeking faith is to be especially callous and vicious. Against
this, the Bible is particularly stern. In sum, a "Bajour" as shown
on the Broadway stage, may be entirely entertaining; in real
life it is more than a "gyp". It is a grievous sin.

b. Under the Cloak of Religion

"Tambourines to Glory"

Text: And the priest shall make atonement for the most
holy place,
and he shall make atonement for the tent of meeting,
and for the altar; and he shall make atonement for
the priests,
and for all the people of the assembly.
—Leviticus 16:33

The High Priest performing his duties on the Day of Atonement had to make atonement for the Sanctuary itself! One can
understand easily such a necessity for the ordinary laymen who
because of their households could require purification by the
priest. That such atonement should be necessary for the very
Temple and its altar—along with the High Priest and his household and fellow priests—appears indeed strange.

The strangeness wears off, however, the more one thinks of it.
The Biblical lawgiver with infinite wisdom understood that the
sanctuary itself might fall short of being what it should be. The
priests and their families, being human, might very easily commit errors. Therefore, it was decreed, that on the Day of Atonement, the Holy Place and those dedicated to the service of the
Lord needed purification even as the rest of the people.

This thought of the necessity of examining and purifying our
religious institutions and practices is brought home more than
half-humorously but none the less sincerely by the Broadway
production, "Tambourines to Glory". Written by Langston
Hughes as a gospel singing play, it is based on his novel.

The story revolves around "Tambourine Temple" which had

been set up by a couple in Harlem for the purpose of preying upon the sinners who entered into it to pray for forgiveness and salvation. Although the locale is Harlem, and the expression is definitely that of Negro people—the singing is beautiful—the message applies everywhere and always. As one character puts it, "Religion has no business being made into a gyp." Yes, indeed, even tambourines require tuning.

8. Old Style Religion's Value

In discussing how religion as belief and practice has been both used and abused, it is in place to consider an interesting case which has been presented as an off-Broadway production.

"Trumpets of the Lord"

Text: All my bones say: "Lord, who is like unto Thee,
Who deliverest the poor from him that is too strong for him,
Yea, the poor and the needy from him that spoileth him?"

—Psalms 35:10

An unusual entertainment is provided by the actors performing in "Trumpets of the Lord" at the off-Broadway theatre, One Sheridan Square. The all-Negro cast offers songs and sermons in the style of the itinerant preachers.

Based on a poetic work, "Trombones of the Lord" by James Weldon Johnson, this piece renamed "Trumpets of the Lord" revolves around the way that the old-time Negro preachers were delivering God's message to their flocks. It must be noted that their interpretation of the Bible was thoroughly anthropomorphic. As such of course, their views fall short of being acceptable. God is not to be considered in such humanistic terms.

This does not mean to say, however, that their preachments were valueless. Speaking to their fellow Negroes who were deprived of education and of human dignity, they spoke to them in a language and style which were understandable. Around these sermons was a ritual of songs and spirituals which made for powerful religious expression.

Whether as trumpets or trombones, these preachers in their

sermons succeeded in passing current with their people. There was an electricity about their very bodies which gave a charge to their words. Those who heard them were moved spiritually and physically, too. Challenged or comforted, bemused or bewitched, the congregants would sing along, dance along and be exalted together with their preachers.

The greatness of the performers at One Sheridan Square is that they succeed in catching and conveying that spirit. In the process, the little theatre achieves the character of a church, and the audience becomes a congregation. This is not an ordinary congregation, however, but one whose very bodies are quickened to declare God's praise.

D. LIFE AND DEATH

1. Be a Man!

The design for living must include a pattern for death. Into this must always be woven the element of courage.

"Soldier in the Rain"

Text: Now the days of David drew nigh that he should die;
        and he charged Solomon, his son, saying:
        "I go the way of all the earth;
        be thou strong therefore, and show thyself a man".
                                          —I Kings 2:12

"Soldier in the Rain" is a motion picture featuring Jackie Gleason and Steve McQueen. Other players in the film are Tuesday Weld and Tom Poston.

With such a cast, one might expect that the movie be a comedy. This it is in an unmistakable and enjoyable fashion. Yet along with its comic quality, "Soldier in the Rain" carries a serious and important message.

Although in no direct sense is the film a "message-piece", yet its very title would be meaningless without recognition of the idea it conveys. It derives its name from a scene in which Steve McQueen dashes through the rain to visit his Army buddy, Jackie Gleason, who has been taken to a hospital following what proves to be a mortal heart seizure.

Following the death of his friend, the master sergeant, Steve McQueen in the picture, reveals a new maturity and acceptance of his place in the world he knows. This is a desirable change from his earlier encounter with death when he lost control of himself.

The point thus made in the film is a reflection of what King David is reported to have told Solomon, his son, when the aged monarch felt that his son would soon be orphaned. To prepare him for the anguish of that day, the king counselled him to be strong.

Most everyone in the course of life and death becomes sooner or later "a soldier in the rain". In dealing with death, we must bear in mind that while we cannot control it in the last instance, we must face it with courage. For each of us, then, there is just one order of the day: "Be a man!"

2. Life and Death—For What?

What man lives for—and what he dies for (and puts others to death for)—only too frequently and sadly points up the irrationality of human existence.

"Pantagleize"

Text: There is that imagineth himself rich,
            yet hath nothing;
         There is that imagineth himself poor,
            yet hath great wealth.
                                        —Proverbs 13:7

Michel de Ghelderode died a few years ago. He was a Belgian playwright who has been called the father of the modern so-called theatre of the absurd.

It was not until after his death, however, that recognition has been accorded his plays as being outstanding artistic creations.

The other week in the Wollman Theatre at Columbia University one of his works, "Pantagleize" was given its New York premiere. Produced and presented by the Columbia Players, it was excellently done. Most of the credit for this is no doubt due to the young, gifted director, Isaiah Sheffer.

Mr. Sheffer succeeded in eliciting from his cast the difficult artistry to fulfill de Ghelderode's description of "Pantagleize" as "a farce to make you sad".

All in all, the play deals with the claims and reactions of revolutionaries and those who would maintain the status quo. Caught in the cross-fire of these antagonists is a poetic soul, Pantagleize, whose strange name emphasizes his bewilderment and naivete in the midst of all the shooting and the shouting. Within him, there is only the longing to live at peace, and to appreciate the simple, though great joys of mere existence.

This kind of yearning points up the false values involved in the social conflict which may lead to disenchantment, frustration and destruction. The Bible knew well this sophisticated mix-up of true values, and pleaded against it.

Pantagleize similarly put it succinctly when upon examining some jewels he exclaims to his beloved: "Vanity! I would much rather have brought you rarer things, a moonbeam, a necklace of dew, the secret of perpetual motion; but you don't find these things in the safes of banks."

It is the life and death struggle for vanities that renders the human experience a "farce to make you sad".

3.   Great Art and Immortality

In the belief in immortality there is more than just hope in life after death. There is expectation that what is wrong here will be ultimately righted. Also, there is the faith that life is not meaninglessly cut off, but has a continuance which redeems it. We may see in great art an entree into an un-ending future life.

"Lord Pengo"

Text: Thou shalt not make for thyself any graven image.
                                                —Exodus 20:4

The second of the Ten Commandments specifically forbade the Hebrews from making idols. This prohibition was then extended naturally to discourage development not only of sculpting, but also of all forms of painting and drawing. Especially was the human form regarded as "verboten" as a subject for artistic treatment.

On this basis we can understand the lack of art in its pictorial aspects in synagogues to this day. Interestingly though, archaeology has uncovered proof that ancient synagogues did have murals. But by and large, it is fair to say that the Old Testament fiat—"Thou shalt make no graven image"—has been the rule that has discouraged the graphic arts in the Hebrew saga.

In the light of this, the recent Broadway play, "Lord Pengo" takes on added interest. The stage character, Lord Pengo, is based on the real-life personality, Lord Duveen. Indeed, S.N. Behrman, the author of the play, also authored a biography of Lord Duveen. The latter, as is the fictional Lord Pengo, was an art connoisseur and salesman par excellence. Both proclaim their aim to be to make America art conscious. This goal interestingly is the national policy of the Kennedy Administration.

This fact highlights how far art has developed over the centuries in the western world, even though the Bible originally discouraged it. Who does not know of the great paintings that have been motivated religiously? In the play, Lord Pengo underscores the simple truth that civilization has been enriched through its artists. From all of this we are reminded that what the Bible objected to was the pagan use of art, not art itself.

Lord Pengo, with his star salesmanship ability, sells works of art to rich clients as insurance against the ravages of death. He tells them that to link their names with undying artistic creations is to achieve a kind of immortality. He happens to be right.

4. Life's Special Wisdom

Everyone cannot be a great artist, or even associate his life with great art, in the usual sense. Everyone, however, can perfect himself in the art of living. It is a most difficult art—whose very worthwhileness often eludes us. This is why we need to turn to our artists and playwrights—and the Book of Books which contains the wisdom of the art of living—for direction when we tend to wander and wonder.

"The Three Sisters"

Text: Vanity of vanities, all is vanity . . .
        What profit hath man of all his labor? . . .
        Our generation passeth away and another generation
            cometh . . .
        There is no rememberance of them of former times.
        The end of the matter: fear God . . .
                            —Ecclesiastes 1:2–4, 12:13

It has been said with good reason that a man's laugh may be
at times more bitter than his cry. For all of that, a laugh has
the power to set things in proportion. By laughing even at one's
self one feels that one should not be overwhelmed by whatever
may happen.

Anton Chekov, the famous Russian dramatist, insisted that
his play, "The Three Sisters", was intended as a comedy. It is
indeed what he intended it to be, for it is in essence an expose
of aspects of the human comedy, of life itself.

Chekov had to insist, however, upon his designation of his
play as a comedy for the natural reaction is to consider it otherwise. It has all the earmarks of the deepest tragedy. It is an
unusually moving presentation of frustration as experienced by
and with the heroïnes of the play, three Russian sisters.

With his typical simple language, which achieves a remarkable moving power, and utilizing symbols such as oak trees,
migratory birds, carnival people, and a fire, Chekov's "The
Three Sisters" reveals the fundamentally disappointing character of so much of human striving. Most capably acted by the
Actors Studio at the Morosco Theatre, the spirit as well as the
message of the playwright shine forth.

Happiness, he tells us, is no proper human goal. Culture,
even when acquired is really useless. Truth in the sense of an
understanding of the meaning of the universe and all that is
in it, must always elude us. There is hardly anything truly good,
for there is always a flaw in it.

What then, is the wisdom of life? It is simply to live, but to
do so with faith that it is all worthwhile. In this, the wisdom
of "The Three Sisters" echoes the wisdom of King David's son.

5. Unseen Forces

Whatever knowledge we may individually and collectively amass, the fact is that there are always left great areas of the unknown, and the mysterious. Part of the very special wisdom of life is to realize that there are invisible forces all about us, affecting our lives. Our faith would have us believe that the universe is friendly to us through life and death—and that unseen forces come to our rescue when we are weary and despairing. Through them we are helped to regain our strength and our salvation.

"My Three Angels"

Text: And Jacob sent messengers before him to Esau, his brother, unto the land of Seir, the field of Edom.
—Genesis 32:4

In the original Hebrew, the Bible uses the word which means "angels" when it speaks of the "messengers" who were dispatched by Jacob to placate his brother, Esau. That the human agents of Jacob were really angels is one of the familiar comments on this text.

This idea may be taken to refer to the human situation in several ways. There is, first, the notion that when a person is engaged in doing what is right, heavenly forces come to his aid. Thus the human messengers who ran Jacob's errand were divinely inspired to do his bidding well. They were, in this sense, angels. Second, there is the concomitant idea that evil may be expected to come to naught by the intervention of supernatural forces which may appear in human form to thwart it. In the case of Jacob and Esau, the messengers sent by Jacob had the divine task to render Esau's vengeance null and void.

In a recent presentation of the comedy "My Three Angels" at the Playhouse on the Mall, this Biblical idea came to mind. The story tells of three convicts who are permitted in a French penal colony to work in a private home. While there, they thwart a villain. They undo a mismatched love affair. They set things right for the householder and his wife, who because of the former's kindly and innocent spirit, might have been victimized.

Frankly, questions could be raised about some of the "angels' " methods. The fundamental point made humorously and well, however, is that there are mysterious forces at work which come to a good man's rescue. Significantly, at the close of the play, which takes place at Christmas time, the prisoner-angels climb a ladder to the roof.

Yes, Virginia, there is a Santa Claus—and much, much more.

Epilogue

Through chapter after chapter, we have watched the Bible have something to offer in the way of instruction and inspiration in each of the areas of a man's life as portrayed on the stages of today's theatre.

The fact that the Bible has so much relevance today is a remarkable thing. The Bible, through its relationship to the theatre, in our day has proven itself to be an ethical and spiritual treasury, rich enough to supply our failing resources of morality and theology. The Bible, we have seen through our six chapters replete with material of life as reflected in the contemporary drama, teaches more than just theology; it teaches a way of life.

Of course—and this is all the more remarkable—very, very few of today's playwrights, to say the most, set themselves to expounding Biblical truths. Yet these doctrines, like the bones of the body, evolved in and out of their works almost as the outcome of the life-process itself. The Biblical verses and citations—indeed the Bible itself—as we consider the "stuff" of today's plays, emerge as if of themselves to give firmness, stability and definiteness to the whole material. Broadway could not maintain itself without the Bible no more than any spiritual life is possible without its truths.

Still a word of caution I feel is in place here. While it is true that there can be a Bible without Broadway, but no Broadway without the Bible, one should not become fanatic, or obscurantist, through one's reverence for the Scriptures.

It has been well-said that he who knows only one book, the Bible, does not even know that. To know any one thing—even the Bible—you must see its relationships to other things, such other things as plays are made of—the stuff of life.

From the trialogue between life, and the Bible and Broadway, can come the renewed realization that life itself is a wondrous theatre, in which the drama of eternity is being played most often beyond human comprehension.

Appendices

A
Plays and Movies Discussed

171

B

Books of the Bible and Verses Cited